Workbook

BACKPACK 4

Second Edition

Mario Herrera · Diane Pinkley

Contributing Writer
Donna Schaffer

PEARSON
Longman

Backpack 4, Second Edition
Workbook

Pearson Education, 10 Bank Street, White Plains, NY 10606, USA

Staff credits: The people who made up the *Backpack 4* Workbook team, representing editorial, production, design, and manufacturing, are Rhea Banker, Carol Brown, Sarah Bupp, Iris Candelaria, Tracey Cataldo, Gina DiLillo, Christine Edmonds, Lucille M. Kennedy, Maria Pia Marrella, Linda Moser, Diane Pinkley, Edie Pullman, Nicole Santos, Susan Saslow, and Andrew Vaccaro.
Text composition: TSI Graphics
Text font: 14 pt HSP Helvetica Text
Illustration credits: Bergstein, David, 4,12, 24, 45, 53, 65, 74; Luis Briseño, 7–8; Catusanu, Mircea, 35; Crane, Jack, 8, 22, 23, 43, 63; Fasolino, Peter, 7, 25, 34, 42, 57, 73; Klug, Dave, 5, 14, 28, 33, 44, 48, 61, 72, 77; Stefflbauer, Thomas, 13
Photo Credits l = left, c = center, r = right, t = top, b = bottom
Page 2 (tl) ©Ken Fisher/Stone/Getty Images, (tcl) ©Doug Menuez/Getty Images, (tcr) Shutterstock.com, (tr) ©Rob/Fotolia; 6 ©Corbis; 16 ©G.K & Vicki Hart/Getty Images; 36 ©Dorling Kindersley Picture Library; 54 Fotolia.com; 76 ©Corbis; 85 (tr) ©Mickey Pfleger/Photo 20-20/PictureQuest, (tr) ©Pierre Burnaugh/PhotoEdit, Inc.; 86 (tr) ©Jennie Woodcock; Reflections/Corbis, (cr) ©Wally McNamee/Corbis; 88 ©Syracuse Newspapers/Al Campanie/The Image Works.
ISBN-13: 978-0-13-245167-3
ISBN-10: 0-13-245167-0

PEARSON LONGMAN ON THE WEB

Pearsonlongman.com offers online resources for teachers and students. Access our Companion Websites, our online catalog, and our local offices around the world.

Visit us at **pearsonlongman.com**.

Contents

Friends Old and New

1 **Listen. Write the missing words.**

blue	brown
curly	different
longer	shorter
straight	taller

Is That You?

Is that you?
I think that you were in my class last year.
You were sitting there; I was sitting here.
But you don't look the same.

Your hair was _____ then

and it was _____ and _____.

Now your hair is _____,

and _____ all around!

Didn't you wear glasses?

And weren't your eyes _____?

Now you're so much _____,

I can't believe it's you.

(Chorus)

Wow, you're really _____,

but I'm glad to see you, Millie.

What? That's not your name?

Now I feel really silly!

(Chorus)

2 **Write. Use words from the box. You will use some words more than once.**

 1
 2
 3
 4

1. Yoko has _____, _____ hair.

2. Paul has _____, _____ hair.

3. Manuel has _____, _____ hair.

4. Elena has _____, _____ hair.

| curly |
| long |
| short |
| straight |

3 **Complete the chart about your classmates. Write complete sentences.**

Who has green eyes?

Melissa has green eyes.

Find someone with . . .	Name
green eyes	Melissa has green eyes.
glasses	
red hair	
brown eyes	
curly brown hair	
short, straight dark hair	
curly blond hair	
blue eyes	
long, straight blond hair	

Who is old**er**? Marco or Emilio?	Emilio is old**er than** Marco.	old → older
Who is young**er**? Marco or Emilio?	Marco is young**er than** Emilio.	young → younger

4 **Draw your family.**

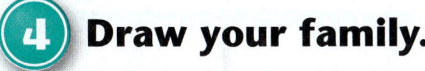

5 **Write about your family. Answer the questions with complete sentences.**

1. Who is older than you?

_____

2. Who is taller than you?

_____

3. Who is younger than you?

_____

4. Who has shorter hair than you?

_____

5. Who wears glasses?

_____

Grammar

When do	they you	**get excited**?	They You	**get excited** when their team wins.		
When does	he she	**get scared**?	He She	**gets scared** when	he she	watches that movie.

6 Answer the questions.

1. When does she get upset?

   _____

   _____

2. When does he get excited?

   _____

   _____

3. When do they get sad?

   _____

   _____

7 Write questions or answers.

1. When do you get upset?

   _____

2. _____

   She gets impatient when her friends are late.

3. When do you get excited?

   _____

4. _____

   They get happy when they win the race.

5. When do you get scared?

   _____

4

8 **Find and circle the words.**

angry	excited	happy	impatient
sad	scared	upset	

S	C	A	R	E	D	D	L	B
R	J	O	S	X	Y	S	A	D
L	S	H	A	C	F	G	R	Y
T	X	A	L	I	B	K	A	B
I	M	P	A	T	I	E	N	T
E	U	P	S	E	T	Z	G	Y
K	A	Y	A	D	T	A	R	L
D	U	O	T	R	E	U	Y	I

When do you get impatient?

When I can't find something right away!

9 **Complete the chart. Ask two friends.**

When do you get _____?	Name _____	Name _____
1. impatient	when she can't find something right away!	
2. happy		
3. excited		
4. sad		
5. upset		
6. scared		

Read *Friends Forever: A Magazine for Kids.*

Are You a Good Friend?

 Complete the sentences.

1. Good friends get excited when _____.

2. Good friends say "I'm sorry" when _____.

3. Good friends listen to their friends when _____.

4. Good friends do not tell others _____.

5. Good friends do things _____.

Our Readers' Letters

 Write a letter to *Friends Forever* about a special friend of yours.

- Use the first letter in the magazine as a model.

- Describe your friend.

- Draw or glue a picture of your friend in the box.

_____

_____

_____

_____

_____

_____

_____

_____

12 Read. Listen and write.

1. Brad is the _____ boy with the blue cap.

2. Her brother is _____ than her friend's brother.

3. Her math book is _____ than her little brother's book.

4. He gets _____ when dinner isn't ready.

5. She gets _____ when she sees a spider.

13 A. Complete the chant. Use words from the box. Listen to check.

A True Friend

A true friend is _____

    and makes you laugh.

A true friend shows you how to do math.

A true friend remembers your birthday.

A true friend helps you in every way.

A true friend is _____

    and doesn't get _____.

A true friend listens

    when you feel _____.

What I'm saying

    is really true.

And there isn't a friend

_____ than you!

funny	kind	mad	sad	truer

B. Write new lines for the chant.

A true friend is _____ and doesn't get _____.

A true friend _____ when you feel _____.

Unit 1

7

Writing

Descriptive Sentences

Good writing has details and descriptions. Use **adjectives** and **comparative forms** of adjectives to make your sentences interesting.

- You can use adjectives to describe people.
  Wanda is **tall**.
  Wanda has **brown** eyes.
  Wanda has **long, blond** hair.
  Wanda is a **happy, friendly** person.
- You can use comparative forms of adjectives to describe similarities and differences between people.
  Wanda is **taller than** I am.
  I am twelve years old. Wanda is thirteen. Wanda is **older than** I am.

Writing Assignment

Using the following steps, you will write sentences describing a family member, a friend, or another person you know. Be sure to describe what the person looks like. Describe the person's personality, too. In your description, you will use adjectives and comparative forms of adjectives.

14 Brainstorm ideas.

- Who do you want to write about?
- What is special about that person?
- Which adjectives describe that person?
- What do you have in common with that person?
- How are you different from that person?

15 Use a T-chart.

Think about the person you want to write about. What do you have in common? How are you different? Use a T-chart to organize the details. On one side of the T-chart, list things that describe you. On the other side of the chart, list things that describe the family member, friend, or other person you want to write about.

Me	Amanda
short hair	long hair
brown eyes	blue eyes
short	tall
funny	serious

Me	
	(person's name)

To help you...

Adjectives:

big	blond	blue	brown	dark	friendly	funny
green	happy	kind	long	old	popular	red
serious	short	shy	small	smart	straight	tall

16 Write.

Use your T-chart to help you write your sentences.

_____

_____

_____

_____

_____

Review

 Look. Answer each question with a complete sentence.

1. Who is taller?

   _____

2. Who has longer hair?

   _____

3. Who has bigger feet?

   _____

4. Who has a smaller nose?

   _____

5. Who has bigger ears?

   _____

| excited | impatient | mad | scared | upset |

18 **Finish the letters. Use words from the box. You may use a word more than once.**

1. Dear Sally,

   I get _____ when my friends are late. It isn't fun when we miss part of a game. What can I do?

2. Dear Sally,

   My brother gets _____ when he can't find a toy. His room is a mess! How can I help him?

3. Dear Sally,

   My cousin Paul gets _____ when his team wins. But after the game, he can't eat. And he can't sleep that night. How can we help him?

4. Dear Sally,

   My little sister gets _____ when she doesn't get her way. She cries and jumps up and down. Her face gets red. What can we do?

5. Dear Sally,

   My friend Lisa gets _____ when she sees spiders. She runs away. I like spiders. They make neat webs. I'm not afraid of them. I get _____ when I see a spider. How can I help Lisa?

Communication Activity

Work with a partner: Student A uses this information and Student B turns to page 12.

Student A

A. Ask your partner questions about Maria. Listen and write the answers.

B. Answer your partner's questions about Angelo.

When does Maria get scared?

When she sees a spider.

Feeling	Angelo	Maria
scared	He sees a big dog.	When she sees a spider.
happy	He swims in the lake.	
excited	He wins a race.	
impatient	His brother teases him.	
upset	Animals get hurt.	
shy	He meets new people.	
silly	He forgets someone's name.	
sad	His friends move away.	

Students work with partners to ask and answer questions. Student A uses the information on page 11 and Student B uses the information on page 12. Students use the conversation shown as a model. Students use their partner's answers to complete the activity. This procedure should be used for other similar Communication Activities at the end of the units in this workbook.

Communication Activity

Work with a partner: Student B uses this information and Student A turns to page 11.

Student B

A. Answer your partner's questions about Maria.

B. Ask questions about Angelo. Listen and write the answers.

Feeling	Angelo	Maria
scared	When he sees a big dog.	She sees a spider.
happy		She plays soccer.
excited		She sees circus animals.
impatient		Her brother is late for the school bus.
upset		She loses something.
shy		She has to talk in front of the class.
silly		She does the wrong homework.
sad		Her sister will not play with her.

It's About Time

1 Listen. Write the missing words.

Tomo's Week

1. What does Tomo do on Monday?

   On Monday Tomo _____ his bed.

2. What does Tomo do on Tuesday?

   On Tuesday Tomo _____ dishes

   and then _____ them away.

3. What does Tomo do on Wednesday?

   On Wednesday Tomo _____ his

   drums from five to six.

   Then he _____ the family dog and

   _____ it new tricks.

4. What does Tomo do on Thursday?

   On Thursday he _____ out the

   garbage, and sometimes _____

   the floor.

5. What does Tomo do on Friday?

   On Friday Tomo _____ to the store

   for all his family's needs.

2 Read. Answer each question with a complete sentence.

Every Saturday morning, Lulu goes to her piano lesson. Then she calls to get phone messages from her friends. Here are the messages her friends left.

- Hi, Lulu. It's Nancy. Guess what I'm doing this afternoon? I'm riding my bike in the park. Do you want to come?

- Hi! It's Molly. I'm going on a hike this afternoon at the park. Do you want to come?

- Hi, Lulu. It's Sue. I'm playing in a concert this afternoon. It's at the park. Do you want to come?

- Hi, Lulu. It's Berta. After I clean my room, I'm meeting some friends at the park. Do you want to come?

- Hi, Lulu. It's Jane. I have to do the dishes. Then I'm going to a picnic in the park. Do you want to come?

- Hi! It's Pam. After I fix my bike, I'm taking it to the park. Do you want to come?

1. What is Nancy doing this afternoon?

   _____

2. What is Molly doing?

   _____

3. What is Sue doing?

   _____

4. What is Berta doing after she cleans her room?

   _____

5. What is Jane doing after she does the dishes?

   _____

6. What is Pam doing after she fixes her bike?

   _____

7. Where do you think Lulu will go this afternoon? Why?

   _____

Hi, Lulu, it's Jane. I have to do the dishes. Then I'm going to a picnic in the park. Do you want to come?

14

| What does | he
she | do in | his
her | free time? | He
She | plays the piano. |
| What do | you
they | do in | your
their | free time? | I
They | paint. |

3 **Read. Write the answers.**

1. What does Omar do in his free time?

_____

2. What does Sheila do in her free time?

_____

3. What do they do in their free time?

_____

4 **Read the chart. Answer the questions with words from the box.**

| every day | once a week | three times a week | twice a week |

		S	M	T	W	T	F	S
Jan	make bed	✗	✗	✗	✗	✗	✗	✗
Tomás	wash dishes		✗		✗		✗	
Jill and Ann	shop for food			✗				✗
Esteban	wash car							✗

1. How often does Jan make her bed?

_____

2. How often does Tomás wash the dishes?

_____

3. How often do Jill and Ann shop for food?

_____

4. How often does Esteban wash the car?

_____

5 Read about Sue. Put the events in order. Four events are done for you.

Sue's Busy Days

Every day is a busy day for Sue. She helps out at the school library before her first class. She eats lunch at noon. Every morning, Sue gets up and brushes her teeth. After her last class, she practices soccer with her team. After lunch, Sue goes to her last three classes. Then she helps her mother make dinner. Then Sue waits for the bus to take her to school. Then she goes for a walk before breakfast. Sue eats dinner at 6:00. After breakfast, she feeds her parrot. After soccer, she goes home. After dinner, Sue does her homework.

1. *Sue gets up and brushes her teeth.*

2. _____

3. _____

4. *Then Sue waits for the bus to take her to school.*

5. _____

6. _____

7. _____

8. *After her last class, she practices soccer with her team.*

9. _____

10. _____

11. *Sue eats dinner at 6:00.*

12. _____

6 Unscramble the word. Write the word.

laencs

1. On Saturdays, Lee _____cleans_____ his room.

esahws

2. After breakfast, he _____ the dishes.

scoko

3. Once a week, he _____ dinner with his mother.

rteacpics

4. He _____ the piano for 30 minutes every day.

skmae

5. Lee _____ his bed every morning.

lpays

6. Lee _____ soccer on weekends.

tsays

7. Lee _____ after school twice a week for extra help with math.

sego

8. Lee _____ for a walk every day.

To Do

✓ Clean my room.
✓ Go for a walk.
✓ Wash the dishes.
_____
_____
_____
_____

7 Write about yourself. Use each unscrambled word from Exercise 6 in a complete sentence.

1. _I clean my room every afternoon._____

2. _____

3. _____

4. _____

5. _____

6. _____

7. _____

8. _____

Read *Kids' Corner Magazine.*

 Read and circle.

Cows Have Good Taste

1. Daniel helps his father milk cows **every morning** / (every afternoon).

2. They **usually** / **always** listen to music when they milk cows.

Ask Alicia

3. The writer's brother has to feed the cat **every day** / **every week**.

4. The writer's brother has to water the plants **twice a week** / **twice a month**.

5. He **sometimes** / **always** forgets to do his chores.

Are You Mother's Little Helper?

 **Enter the contest in *Kids' Corner Magazine.***

Write a letter to the magazine. Answer these questions:

• Do you help around the house?

• What chores do you do?

• How often do you do them?

_____

_____

_____

_____

_____

_____

_____

_____

_____

 **Listen and write.**

1. Laura has a piano lesson ___once a week_____.
   a. twice a week   b. once a week

2. She stays with her cousin for an hour _____.
   a. on Tuesdays and Thursdays   b. every morning

3. Ken takes out the garbage _____.
   a. on Saturday   b. every day

4. He helps his dad wash the car _____.
   a. twice a month   b. once a week

5. The English Club meets _____.
   a. twice a week   b. every Friday

 **A. Listen. Write the missing words.**

A Kid's Life

1. We _____ scooters or _____ ball.

2. We _____ shopping at the mall.

3. We _____ books and magazines.

4. We _____ at computer screens.

5. We _____ oak trees or _____ jacks.

6. We _____ yummy, healthy snacks.

7. We _____ our bedrooms and
   _____ the cats.

8. We _____ away our baseball bats.

9. We always _____ as mother asks!

B. Write about you. What do you do in your free time? Name two activities.

_____

_____

Unit 2

19

Writing

Compound Sentences

A **compound sentence** is one longer sentence made up of two **simple sentences**. You can use *and, but,* or *or* to connect the two shorter sentences together.

- Use *and* to show the connected ideas are similar.

two simple sentences
On Thursday Tomo takes out the garbage.   On Thursday Tomo sweeps the floor.
one compound sentence
On Thursday Tomo takes out the garbage, **and** he sweeps the floor.

- Use *but* to show the connected ideas are different.

two simple sentences
Keisha likes soccer.   Keisha doesn't like to play tennis.
one compound sentence
Keisha likes soccer, **but** she doesn't like to play tennis.

- Use *or* to show a choice between the connected ideas.

two simple sentences
Roberto plays the drums after school.   Roberto rides his bike after school.
one compound sentence
Roberto plays the drums, **or** he rides his bike after school.

Are these sentences simple or compound? Circle S for *simple* or C for *compound*.

My sister plays chess after school.   S   C

I like checkers, but I don't like chess.   S   C

Katia washes the dishes on weekends.   S   C

Jon feeds the cat or takes out the garbage every evening.   S   C

20

Writing Assignment

Using the following steps, you will write compound sentences describing some of your family's or your friends' activities. In your sentences, use *and, but,* and *or.*

 Brainstorm ideas.

- Who do you want to write about?
- What activities do the people like to do?
- What activities don't the people like to do?
- When do the people do the activities?

 Use a sentence-combining chart.

Think about the people and activities you will write about. Use a sentence-combining chart to help you form compound sentences.

Leo sings in a group. + Leo plays in a band. = Leo sings in a group, and he plays in a band.

Simple Sentence	and, but, or	Simple Sentence
Leo sings in a group.	and	Leo plays in a band.
	and	
	but	
	or	

┌─ **To help you...** ─────────────────────────────────

Activities:

feed the cat	go to the store	make the bed	play chess
play the piano	play a video game	sweep the floor	take out the garbage
walk the dog	wash the car	wash the dishes	work in the garden

 **Write.**

Use your sentence-combining chart to write your compound sentences here.

_____

_____

_____

Review

15 **Write questions or answers.**

1. How often do you brush your teeth?

   _____

2. _____

   Melissa and Susan ride their bikes three times a week.

3. How often do you go to the movies?

   _____

4. _____

   John and his family go on vacation twice a year.

16 **Write. Complete the sentences. Use words from the box.**

| clean |
| make |
| play |
| ride |
| shop |
| sing |
| stay |
| wash |

1. Kevin _____ baseball twice a week.
2. She _____ after school on Wednesday afternoons for help with math.
3. Maria _____ her room every Saturday morning.
4. Kathy _____ jewelry in her free time.
5. Marshall _____ for food on Mondays.
6. They _____ their bikes on weekends.
7. Myra and Mel _____ songs with their group twice a month.
8. Lin _____ the car three times a month.

17 **Write.**

1. What do you like to do in your free time? How often do you do it?

   _____

2. What chores do you do? How often do you do them?

   _____

   _____

22

Communication Activity

Work with a partner: Student A uses this information and Student B turns to page 24.

Student A

A. How often do you do it? Complete the chart.

B. Find a partner. Ask your partner questions. Listen and write the answers.

C. Answer your partner's questions.

What	You: How often?	Your partner: How often?
clean room	Once a week.	Every night.
brush teeth		
go to the movies		
watch TV		
play sports		
make bed		
talk on the phone		
go to the library		
go on vacation		
go _____ shopping		

Communication Activity

Work with a partner: Student B uses this information and Student A turns to page 23.

Student B

A. How often do you do it? Complete the chart.

B. Work with your partner. Answer your partner's questions.

C. Ask your partner questions. Listen and write the answers.

What	You: How often?	Your partner: How often?
clean room	Every night.	Once a week.
brush teeth		
go to the movies		
watch TV		
play sports		
make bed		
talk on the phone		
go to the library		
go on vacation		
go _____ shopping		

At the World's Table

1 **Listen. Write the missing words. Match.**

What's That?

What is that on your plate?
It looks and smells so great!
I would like to try some!

Would you like to try some?

It's a Korean recipe.

It's _____.

It's really good, you'll see!

And would you like to try some?

It's a Mexican recipe.

It's made with _____

Oh try some now, you'll see!

Would you like to try some?

It's a Moroccan recipe

   with _____.

It's really good, you'll see!

And would you like to try some?

It's an Italian recipe.

It's _____.

Oh try some now, you'll see!

hot and spicy cabbage
pasta cooked with meatballs
peppers and tomatoes
rice and chicken

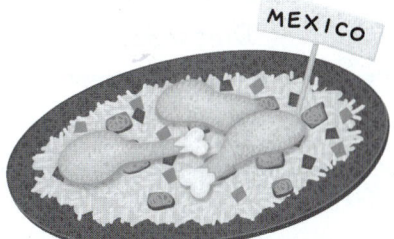

MEXICO

ITALY

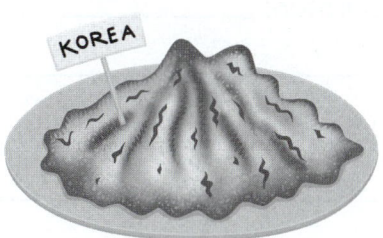

KOREA

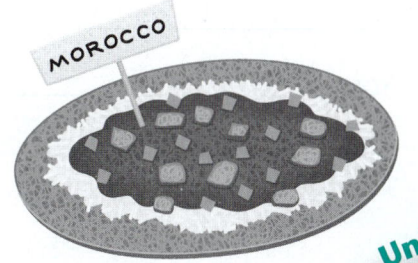

MOROCCO

Read. What would they like to order?
Write. Use *I'd like* and *some*.

Soups
Chicken • Tomato • Vegetable

Sandwiches
Bacon, lettuce, and tomato
Cheese • Chicken • Meatball
Tuna • Turkey

Drinks
Apple juice • Orange juice
Bottled water • Regular soda
Diet soda

Who?	What he or she would like to eat...	What he or she would like to drink...
Carmen	cheese sandwich	diet soda
Jason	bacon, lettuce, and tomato sandwich	apple juice
Jennifer	tuna sandwich tomato soup	bottled water

Waiter: What would you like to order?

Carmen: _____

_____

Jason: _____

_____

Jennifer: _____

_____

You: _____

_____

Grammar

What **would** you **like**?	**I'd like** some pasta.	I'd like → I would like
What **would** he / she **like**?	He'd / She'd **like** a cup of soup.	He'd like → He would like
		She'd like → She would like

3 Complete the sentences.

1. Good morning. What _____ you _____ to order?

2. I _____ a bowl of chicken noodle soup, please.

3. She _____ a hamburger and some fries.

4. He _____ some tuna salad.

Grammar

| **Would** | you he/she you they | **try** tofu? | Yes, | I he/she we they | **would**. | No, | I he/she we they | **wouldn't**. |

4 Complete the sentences.

1. _____ she order the noodles?

   Yes, she _____.

2. _____ she eat tofu?

   No, she _____, but her brother would.

3. _____ they drink the fruit juice?

   Yes, they _____.

4. _____ they eat chili peppers?

   Yes, they _____. They like spicy food!

5. _____ they try sushi?

   No, they _____. They don't like raw fish.

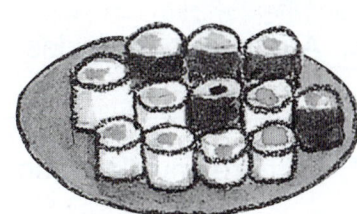

Unit 3

27

5 **Read the menu. Answer the questions.**

Today's Breakfast Menu

<u>Today's Cereal</u>
Oatmeal
<u>Eggs</u>
Ham and eggs
Cheese omelet
<u>Bread</u>
Bagel with cream cheese
Toast with grape jam
<u>Drinks</u>
Orange juice   Tea
Hot chocolate   Coffee

1. Is there any grapefruit juice today?

   No, there isn't any.

2. Is there any ham on the menu today?

   _____

3. Is there any hot chocolate today?

   _____

4. Are there any eggs on the menu today?

   _____

5. Are there any sweet rolls today?

   _____

6 **Look at the foods on sale and answer each question with a complete sentence. Then write your own question and answer.**

1. Is there any vegetable soup on sale today?

   _____

2. Is there any fruit?

   _____

3. Is there any cake on sale?

   _____

4. Is there any stew?

   _____

5. Is there any white rice?

   _____

6. Are there any pickles?

   _____

7. Is there any diet soda?

   _____

8. _____

   _____

SALE 50% OFF

APPLE JUICE   PICKLES   BROWN RICE   Chicken Soup   Beef Stew   POTATOES

<u>Grocery List</u>
Bananas
Cabbage
Chocolate cake
Diet soda
Pickles
Potatoes
Stew
Vegetable soup
White rice

7 Unscramble and write the words on the list. Answer the question by writing the circled letters in order.

Grocery List

1. nisoon   __ __ __ ◯ __ __
2. cbnoa   __ __ __ __ ◯ __
3. esagsuas   __ __ ◯ __ __ __ __
4. babgcae   __ __ __ __ ◯ __ __
5. teeltuc   ◯ __ __ __ __ __ __
6. eotmoast   __ __ __ __ __ __ ◯ __

What do all of the things on the list have in common?

They're all __ __   __ __ __ __!

8 **A. Put the food in the right place on the grocery list.**

apples
bananas
beans
carrots
celery
diet soda
fruit juice
hamburgers
hot dogs
milk
oranges
roast beef

Grocery List

Vegetables   **Fruit**

_____   _____

_____   _____

_____   _____

Drinks   **Meat**

_____   _____

_____   _____

B. Look back at the list in Part A. Check the food you would put on your grocery list. What would you like for snacks? List the food here.

Snacks

_potato chips_____   _____

_____   _____

Food Facts and Fun: A Magazine for Food Fans

Read *Food Facts and Fun: A Magazine for Food Fans.*

What's a Food Pyramid?

(9) **A. Check the correct box.**

1. How much fat should you eat each day?

   ☐ just a little   ☐ 3–5 servings

2. How much milk, yogurt, and cheese should you eat each day?

   ☐ 2–3 servings   ☐ 6–11 servings

3. How much fruit should you eat each day?

   ☐ just a little   ☐ 2–4 servings

4. How much grain, such as bread and rice, should you eat each day?

   ☐ 2–3 servings   ☐ 6–11 servings

Fats, Oils, Sweets (Just a little!)

Milk, Yogurt, Cheese (2–3 servings a day)

Vegetables (3–5 servings a day)

Meat, Poultry, Fish, Eggs, Dry Beans, Nuts (2–3 servings a day)

Fruits (2–4 servings a day)

Bread, Rice, Cereal Grains, Pasta (6–11 servings a day)

B. What are your favorite foods in each group?

1. Grains: _____

2. Vegetables: _____

3. Fruits: _____

4. Meat: _____

5. Milk: _____

(10) **Write about food you would like to have on a menu.**

- Do research about food groups and food that helps people stay in good health.

- Which of these foods do you like?

- Plan and write a menu.

- Write a dialogue about your menu.

  <u>Waiter: What would you like?</u>

  <u>Customer: I'd like some oatmeal.</u>

- Find a partner. Read your dialogue.

Your Menu

Breakfast
<u>oatmeal</u>   _____

Lunch
_____   _____

Dinner
_____   _____

11 **Listen. Circle T for *True* or F for *False*.**

1. He's having bacon and eggs for breakfast.   T   F

2. She's having a sandwich and some olives.   T   F

3. He wants a hamburger and some fries.   T   F

4. Some people like to eat insects.   T   F

5. She'd never eat raw fish.   T   F

12 **Listen and write. Use words from the box.**

I Don't Want To!

bean paste
dumpling
lentil soup
octopus
Roquefort cheese

Now don't be silly, try it.

Just one spoonful, taste it.

If you would try this _____ _____,

     you'd see how much you like it!

Now come on, have a taste.

There's no more time to waste.

If you would try this _____ now,

     you'd see you like _____ _____!

Now come on, have a bite.

Will this take all night?

If you would try this _____,

     you'd know the taste is right!

Now don't be silly, try it.

Just one mouthful, taste it.

If you would try this _____ _____,

     you'd see how much you like it!

Writing

The Paragraph

A paragraph is a group of sentences about one **main idea**. A paragraph looks different from a list of sentences. The first sentence is usually **indented**, or moved in a few spaces. The rest of the sentences in the paragraph form a block of text.

The **topic sentence** tells the main idea of the paragraph. It is usually the first sentence. The other sentences in the paragraph give more information about the main idea. They make up the **body** of the paragraph.

In the paragraph below, which sentence is the topic sentence? Underline it. Which sentences make up the **body** of the paragraph?

> Breakfast is my favorite meal. On school days I like to have a small breakfast. I eat hot oatmeal with milk. On weekends I have a bigger breakfast. I like to start with orange juice. Then I have bacon and eggs and toast with jam. Sometimes on special occasions, I have pancakes with syrup.

Writing Assignment

Using the following steps, you will write a paragraph about your favorite meal. Remember to begin with a topic sentence.

13 Brainstorm ideas.

- What is your favorite meal?
- What foods do you eat for that meal on school days? on weekends? on special occasions?

 **Use a word map.**

A word map can help you organize ideas for your paragraph. Write the name of your topic in the center circle. Write words that give more information about that topic in circles around it.

Complete the word map about your topic. Add more circles if you need them.

┌─ **To help you...** ────────────────────────────────┐
Foods: soups, salads, fruits, vegetables, meats, desserts, drinks
Meals: breakfast, lunch, dinner
└──┘

 **Write.**

Use your word map to help you write your paragraph. Be sure to begin with a topic sentence.

_____

_____

_____

_____

Review

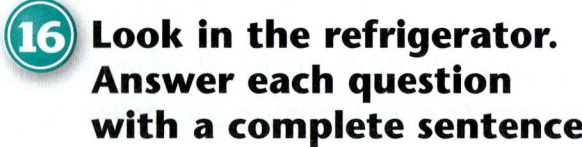

16 **Look in the refrigerator. Answer each question with a complete sentence.**

1. Is there any diet soda?

   _____

2. Is there any apple juice?

   _____

3. Are there any hot dogs?

   _____

4. Is there any lettuce?

   _____

5. Are there any oranges?

   _____

17 **Read the menu. Answer each question with a complete sentence.**

Sally's Sidewalk Café			
Salads			
Lettuce salad	$4.50	Fruit salad	$4.00
Sandwiches			
Cheese	$3.25	Peanut butter	$3.00
Hot dog	$3.50	Hamburger	$5.50
Tuna fish	$4.25	Chicken	$6.00

Desserts			
Ice cream	$2.50	Cherry pie	$3.00
Chocolate cake	$2.50	Rice pudding	$2.00
Drinks			
Tomato juice	$1.50	Soda	$2.00
Orange juice	$1.50	Milk	$1.75

1. Which salad would you like?

   _____

2. Which sandwich would you like?

   _____

3. What would you like for dessert?

   _____

4. What would you like to drink?

   _____

Communication Activity

Work with a partner: Student A uses this information and Student B turns to page 36.

Student A

A. Would you try it? Complete the chart.

B. Find a partner. Ask your partner questions. Listen and write the answers.

C. Answer your partner's questions.

Would you try chili peppers?

Yes, I would. I like spicy food!

Which food?	You	Your partner
chili peppers	No, I wouldn't. I don't like spicy food!	Yes, I would. I like spicy food!
grilled fish		
a Korean dish with hot and spicy cabbage		
a Moroccan dish with peppers and tomatoes		
a Mexican dish with rice and chicken		
an Italian dish with pasta and meatballs		
raw fish		
plantain		

Communication Activity

Work with a partner: Student B uses this information and Student A turns to page 35.

Student B

A. Would you try it? Complete the chart.

B. Work with your partner. Answer your partner's questions.

C. Ask your partner questions. Listen and write the answers.

Would you try chili peppers?

Yes, I would. I like spicy food!

Which food?	You	Your partner
chili peppers	Yes, I would. I like spicy food!	No, I wouldn't. I don't like spicy food!
grilled fish		
a Korean dish with hot and spicy cabbage		
a Moroccan dish with peppers and tomatoes		
a Mexican dish with rice and chicken		
an Italian dish with pasta and meatballs		
raw fish		
plantain		

4 Take Care!

TRACK 12

1 **Listen. Answer each question with a complete sentence. Match.**

Good Advice

1. What should you wear on a bike? Why?

_____

_____

_____

2. Why shouldn't Meg stay up late?

_____

_____

_____

3. What should they do to be safe in the sun? Why?

_____

_____

_____

4. What shouldn't Al do on the ice and snow? Why?

_____

_____

_____

You should take care of yourself!

Read the letters. Choose two. Answer the letters. Give advice. Use *should* and *shouldn't*.

Doctor B. Well writes for a newspaper. People write to her and ask for advice. She tells them what they should and shouldn't do to be well.

Dear Doctor B. Well,

I'm at home with a broken leg. I'm so bored. I eat candy all day. Now I have a toothache.

What should I do?

Upset

Dear Doctor B. Well,

I'm on vacation and have a bad cold. I'm getting a sore throat, too. My mother took my temperature, but I don't have a fever. I have five vacation days left. What should I do to get better?

Impatient

Dear Doctor B. Well,

We are going on a vacation! I like to play out in the sun. Last year I got a bad burn. It ruined my vacation!

What should I do?

Excited

Dear _____

_____

_____

_____

_____

Doctor B. Well

Dear _____

_____

_____

_____

_____

Doctor B. Well

Grammar

I		myself.				
You		yourself.			He	himself.
We	hurt	ourselves.			She	hurt	herself.
You		yourselves.				
They		themselves.				

3 **Complete the sentences. Find each person in the picture. Write each person's name in a box.**

1. Sara didn't wear her helmet and hurt

   _____ on her bike.

2. Ted cut _____ when he fell.

3. Diane and Eva didn't protect

   _____ in the sun.

4. Bill ate too much candy and made

   _____ sick.

5. Polly fell and hurt _____

   on the wet and slippery sidewalk.

4 **Complete the sentences. Then draw one way people can take care of themselves. Write a title.**

1. We take care of _____.
   We wear hats and sunglasses in the sun.

2. Do you take care of _____?
   Do you wear helmets on your bikes?

3. They take care of _____!
   They go to bed early and get plenty of rest.

4. I take care of _____.
   I exercise every day.

_____
(title)

I			I		
You			You		
He		**should** wear a bike helmet.	He		**shouldn't** stay up so late.
She			She		
We			We		
They			They		

5 Complete the sentences. Use *should* or *shouldn't*.

1. Kevin and Lauren _____ eat too many sweets.

2. Polly _____ go to the dentist for her toothache.

3. Sam _____ wear comfortable shoes when he goes for a walk.

4. Gina _____ play soccer without safety equipment.

5. We _____ drink at least six glasses of water a day.

6. You _____ wear sunscreen on sunny days.

7. Sara _____ exercise every day.

8. Ben _____ run fast when it's wet and slippery out.

6 Write five of your own health rules. Use words from the box.
Use *should* or *shouldn't*.

drink lots of soda	drink plenty of water
eat a lot of cake and cookies	eat plenty of fruit and vegetables
get plenty of exercise	ride your bike too fast
watch too much TV	wear a bike helmet

1. _____

2. _____

3. _____

4. _____

5. _____

7 **Look at the pictures. Use them to do the crossword puzzle.**

Down ↓

5.
6.
7.
8.

Across →

1.
2.
3.
4.

8 **Choose five health problems in Exercise 7. Give advice for each. Use words from the box for ideas.**

| aspirin | dentist | doctor | lots of water | plenty | tea |

1. _____

2. _____

3. _____

4. _____

5. _____

Read *Safe and Sound: A Health Magazine for Kids*.

 Circle the correct word.

1. Skyler knew that he **should / shouldn't** act fast to rescue his father and brother.

2. Skyler knew that he **should / shouldn't** stay calm in an emergency.

3. You **should / shouldn't** keep emergency phone numbers with you.

4. A first-aid kit **should / shouldn't** have a thermometer in it.

Our Readers Want to Know . . .

 Pretend that you are a writer for *Safe and Sound: A Health Magazine for Kids*.

- Take a survey at your school. Find out the top reasons kids stay home. Ask teachers, the school nurse, and other students.
- Write your own answer to Hui-mei Wang's letter. Give advice. What can kids at your school do to improve attendance?

Top reasons at my school:

- _____
- _____
- _____
- _____

My advice:

_____
_____
_____
_____
_____

11 **Listen and circle the letter of the correct answer.**

1. What's the matter?
   a. She has a stomachache.   b. She has a toothache.   c. She has a headache.

2. What's the matter?
   a. He has a headache.   b. He has an earache.   c. He has a cold and
                                                       a sore throat.

3. What's the matter?
   a. She has a toothache.   b. She has an earache.   c. She has a headache.

4. What's the matter?
   a. He has a sore throat.   b. He has an earache.   c. He has a stomachache.

12 **Listen and write. Then write what each probably said to Tommy and Cathy.**

Who's Sorry Now?

1. Why is Tommy sick in bed?

   He _____ what his mother said.

2. What did Tommy do to get sick?

   He _____ on his plate.

   He _____ at night.

   And he _____ late.

3. Why is Cathy sick in bed?

   She _____ what her doctor said.

4. What's the matter with Cathy?

   She has _____. Her throat is _____.

   She has _____, _____, and more.

5. How could Cathy and Tommy feel great and fine?

   They could _____ of themselves!

Tommy's Mother

You should _____.

You shouldn't _____.

You shouldn't _____.

Cathy's Doctor

You should _____

of yourself!

Unit 4

43

Writing

Parts of a Paragraph

A paragraph is a group of sentences about one main idea. The **topic sentence**, usually the first sentence in the paragraph, tells the main idea. The other sentences form the body of the paragraph. Sentences that give facts, details, reasons, and examples are called **detail sentences**. If you are writing just one paragraph, it can have a final **concluding sentence** that tells the main idea again in different words. Your paragraph can have a **title** as well.

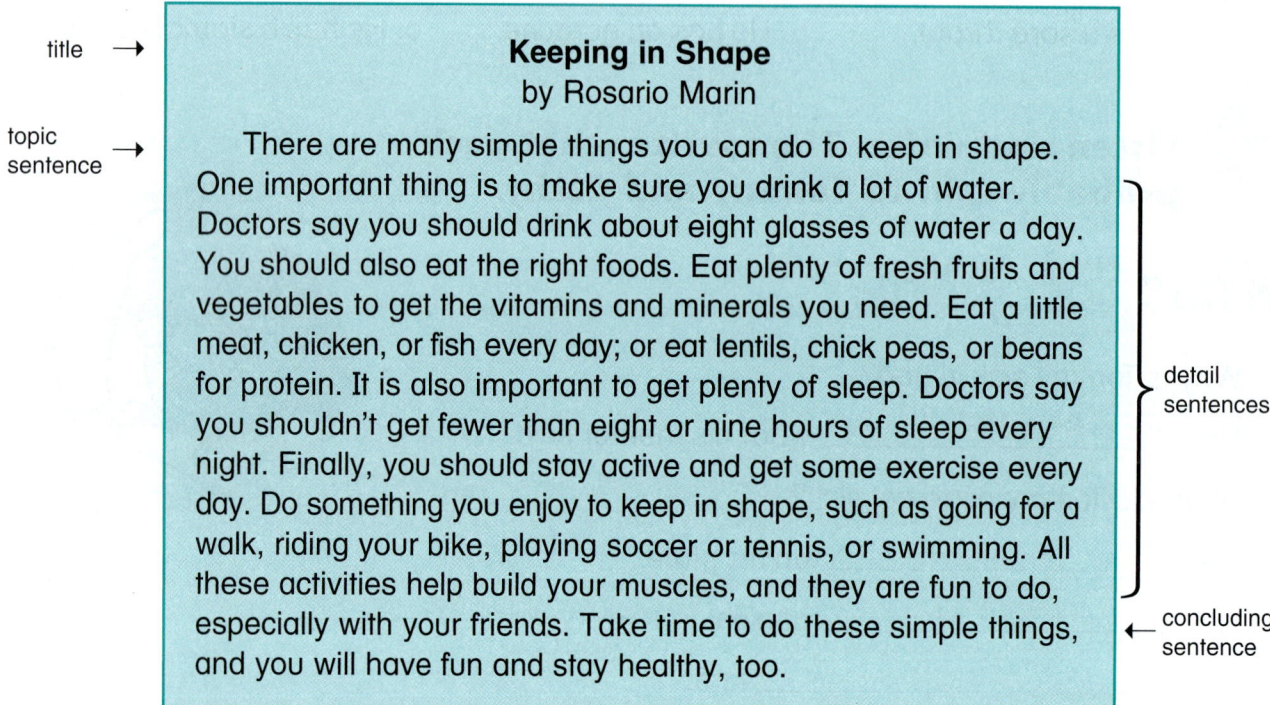

title →

topic sentence →

Keeping in Shape
by Rosario Marin

There are many simple things you can do to keep in shape. One important thing is to make sure you drink a lot of water. Doctors say you should drink about eight glasses of water a day. You should also eat the right foods. Eat plenty of fresh fruits and vegetables to get the vitamins and minerals you need. Eat a little meat, chicken, or fish every day; or eat lentils, chick peas, or beans for protein. It is also important to get plenty of sleep. Doctors say you shouldn't get fewer than eight or nine hours of sleep every night. Finally, you should stay active and get some exercise every day. Do something you enjoy to keep in shape, such as going for a walk, riding your bike, playing soccer or tennis, or swimming. All these activities help build your muscles, and they are fun to do, especially with your friends. Take time to do these simple things, and you will have fun and stay healthy, too.

detail sentences

← concluding sentence

The ten sentences that follow are all sentences in one paragraph about sugar. Read them and then decide which part of the paragraph they are. Circle T for *title,* TS for *topic sentence,* DS for *detail sentence*, or CS for *concluding sentence.*

1. Second, sugar can also hurt your teeth because it can cause cavities and toothaches.   T   TS   DS   CS

2. Finally, too much sugar changes your energy level.   T   TS   DS   CS

3. We all love the sweet taste of sugar, but eating too much sugar can cause serious health problems.   T   TS   DS   CS

4. Too much sugar changes your appetite, too.   T   TS   DS   CS

5. Sugar Isn't as Sweet as We Think   T   TS   DS   CS

6. First, too much candy or desserts full of sugar can cause a bad stomachache.   T   TS   DS   CS

7. At first, the sugar you eat gives you extra energy.	T	TS	DS	CS
8. For example, when you eat a lot of candy, you feel full and then you don't eat good, healthy food.	T	TS	DS	CS
9. For all these reasons, we need to limit the sugar we eat to keep in shape.	T	TS	DS	CS
10. Later, your energy goes away, and you feel tired.	T	TS	DS	CS

Writing Assignment

Using the following steps, you will write a paragraph that includes all the possible parts.

 **Brainstorm ideas.**

- Pick one of these topics or a topic of your own.
  - Playing Safely Outdoors
  - How to Be a Good Friend
  - A Good First-Aid Kit
  - A Healthful Diet
- What details can you use to support your main idea?

(14) Use a paragraph template.

A paragraph template helps you organize your topic sentence, detail sentences, and concluding sentence.

> Title: _____
> Topic sentence: _____
> _____
> Detail sentence: _____
> _____ Detail sentence: _____
> _____
> _____ Detail sentence: _____
> _____
> _____
> Concluding sentence: _____
> _____

 **Write.**

Make your own template to help you organize your paragraph. Then write your paragraph on a separate piece of paper.

┌─ **To help you...** ─────────────────────────────

Editing Tip: Show your paragraph to a friend. Can he or she find your topic sentence? your detail sentences? your concluding sentence?

Review

16 **Complete the sentences. Use *herself*, *himself*, *yourself*, or *themselves*.**

1. They didn't wear equipment to protect _____ when they played soccer. So Bill hurt his knee, and Jack hurt his arm.

2. Lisa was in a hurry to make a sandwich and cut _____ with the knife.

3. Mike forgot to wear his helmet and hurt _____ on his bike.

4. They didn't wear hats and sunglasses and burned _____ on a hot and sunny day.

5. Jennifer! Don't burn _____ on the hot stove.

17 **Read the sentences in Exercise 13. Give advice. Use *should* or *shouldn't*.**

1. _____
   _____

2. _____
   _____

3. _____
   _____

4. _____
   _____

5. _____
   _____

You should take care of yourselves!

Communication Activity

Work with a partner: Student A uses this information and Student B turns to page 48.

Student A

A. How often? How much? Complete the chart.

B. Find a partner. Ask your partner questions. Listen and write the answers. Give advice.

C. Answer your partner's questions.

How often do you exercise?

You should exercise more!

Once a week. I ride my bike on Wednesday afternoon.

Health and Safety Habits	You: How often? / How much?	Your partner: How often? / How much?
Exercise	Every day.	Once a week.
Drink water		
Eat fruit and vegetables		
Eat sweets		
Sleep		
Brush teeth		
Watch TV		
Wear my seatbelt in the car		
Follow other safety rules		

Communication Activity

Work with a partner: Student B uses this information and Student A turns to page 47.

Student B

A. How often? How much? Complete the chart.

B. Work with your partner. Answer your partner's questions.

C. Ask your partner questions. Listen and write the answers. Give advise.

How often do you exercise?

You should exercise more!

Once a week. I ride my bike on Wednesday afternoon.

Health and Safety Habits	You: How often?/ How much?	Your partner: How often?/ How much?
Exercise	Once a week.	Every day.
Drink water		
Eat fruit and vegetables		
Eat sweets		
Sleep		
Brush teeth		
Watch TV		
Wear my seatbelt in the car		
Follow other safety rules		

Animals Past and Present

1 **Listen. Answer the questions.
Use words from the box.**

Dinosaur Days

fast	four	huge	long	meat	millions
plants	short	slow	smaller	taller	two

1. What did dinosaurs look like?

   Some were _____,

   and some were _____.

   Some were _____,

   and some were _____.

2. How quick were they?

   Some were _____,

   and some were _____.

3. How long ago did they live?

   Many _____ of years ago.

4. How did they get around?

   Some walked on _____ legs,

   and some walked on _____.

5. What kind of names did they have?

   They had _____ names.

6. What did they eat?

   Some ate _____,

   and some ate _____.

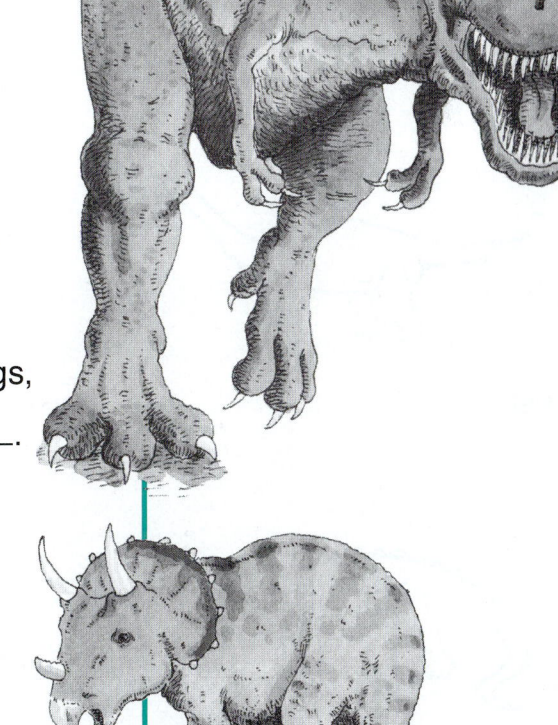

② **Compare the dinosaurs. Write the *-er* form of the word.**

1. small _____

2. tall _____

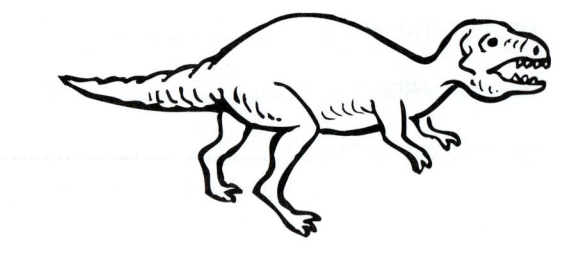

3. heavy _____

4. big _____

5. long _____

What	happened to the Pyrenean ibex?	It died out.
When	did dinosaurs die out?	They died out about 65 million years ago.
Where	did the last Pyrenean ibex live?	It lived in Spain.
How	big were some dinosaurs?	Some were bigger than an elephant.

3 **Write questions. Use each question word once.**

Dodo bird   Passenger pigeon   Steller's sea cow   Moa

1. _____

People ate the Dodo birds' meat, and rats ate their eggs. They died out.

2. _____

The last Passenger pigeon died in 1914.

3. _____

The last sea cow was killed on Bering Island in the North Pacific Ocean.

4. _____

Some Moas were nearly twelve feet (four meters) tall!

Grammar

Why did Steller's sea cows die out?	They died out **because** people hunted them too much.
Why are Komodo dragons endangered?	They are endangered **because** people are hunting them, and they are losing their habitat.

4 **Write answers.**

1. Why did the Pyrenean ibex die out?

_____

2. Why are some animals endangered?

_____

_____

5 **Read the article about dinosaurs. Answer the questions.**

What Happened to the Dinosaurs?

Dinosaurs lived for more than 160 million years! So why did they all die out? Some people think an asteroid hit the Earth and made it too cold for the dinosaurs to live. Others think there were two huge explosions from volcanoes. Each explosion spread ashes all over the Earth. These ashes stayed in the air for many, many years! The explosions changed the climate and made it too hard for the dinosaurs to live.

I. The article gives two ideas about why the dinosaurs died out. What are they?

_____

_____

_____

_____

_____

2. What do you think? Why did the dinosaurs die out?

_____

_____

_____

_____

_____

6 Do the puzzle. Use the simple past.

Across →

1. Some dinosaurs _____ (are) smaller than a hen.
2. Dinosaurs _____ (live) for 160 million years!
3. The habitat of the Pyrenean ibex _____ (disappear).
4. Some animals are extinct because people _____ (hunt) them too much.
5. Maybe an asteroid hit the Earth and _____ (make) it too cold for the dinosaurs to live.

Down ↓

6. Some dinosaurs _____ (walk) on two legs.
7. Dinosaurs _____ (have) long names.
8. The biggest dinosaurs _____ (eat) plants.
9. Dinosaurs _____ (die) out 65 million years ago.
10. Some dinosaurs _____ (grow) to be 75–89 feet (23–27 meters) long!

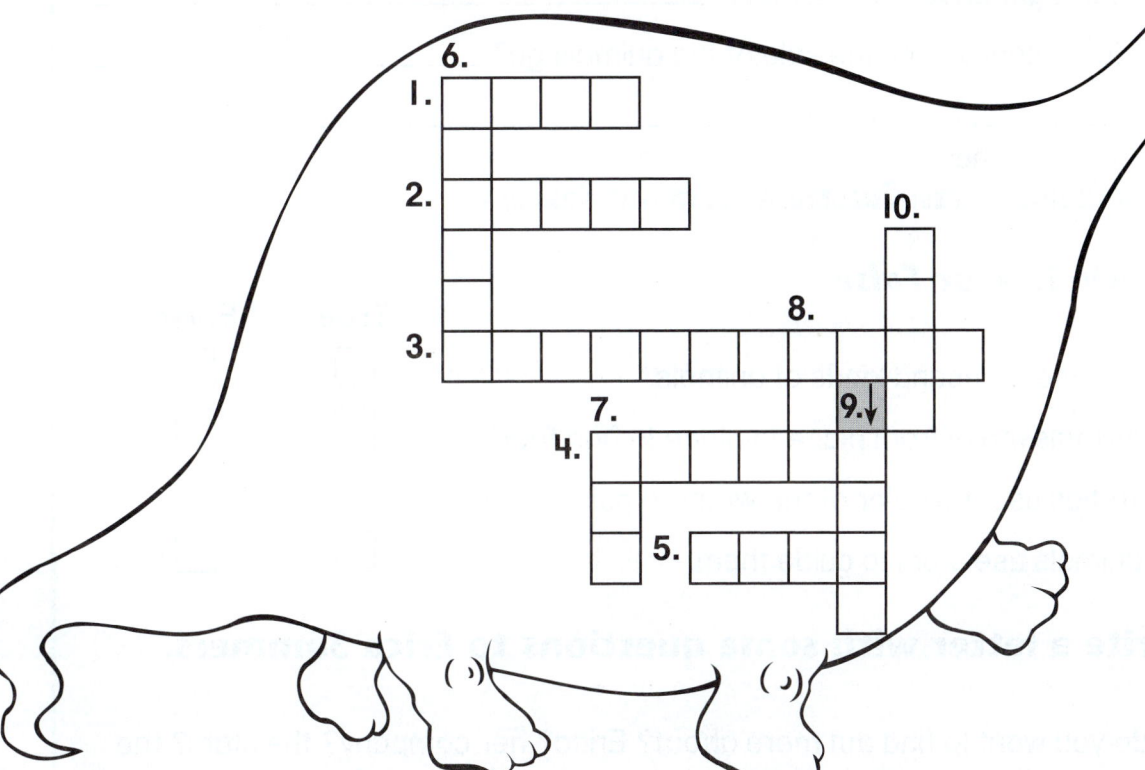

7 Choose four words from the puzzle. Write a sentence using each word.

1. _____

2. _____

3. _____

4. _____

Animal Tracks Magazine

Read *Animal Tracks Magazine: for kids who are wild about animals.*

You're Our Star, Erica!

 Write answers to the questions.

1. What did Erica Summers do? _____

2. How old was she? _____

3. Why does Erica sell the toys? _____

4. What is Erica's company called? _____

5. Who has bought Erica's toy animals? _____

6. Where does money from the sale of the animals go? _____

_____

Fascinating Animal Facts: Questions from Our Readers

9 **Check *True* or *False*.**

	True	False
1. There are one thousand kinds of animals.	☐	☐
2. Some animals move from place to place to find food.	☐	☐
3. Green turtles use the color of the water to guide them.	☐	☐
4. Some animals use stars to guide them.	☐	☐

10 **Write a letter with some questions to Erica Summers.**

• What do you want to find out more about? Erica? her company? the stars? the toy animals?

Question: _____	Question: _____
_____	_____
_____	_____
_____	_____
_____	_____
_____	_____

11 Listen. Circle the letter of the correct answer.

1. Where did many of the really big dinosaurs live?
   a. Argentina   b. The United States

2. Which dinosaur was longer, *Argentinosaurus huinculensis* or *Diplodocus*?
   a. *Argentinosaurus huinculensis*   b. *Diplodocus*

3. Which meat-eating dinosaur, at eight tons, was heavier?
   a. *Tyrannosaurus rex*   b. *Giganotosaurus carolinii*

4. Where did many of the really small dinosaurs live?
   a. China   b. Germany

5. Which dinosaur was smaller and shorter, *Wannanosaurus* or *Compsognathus*?
   a. *Wannanosaurus*   b. *Compsognathus*

12 A. Listen to the chant. Answer each question with a complete sentence.

Animals All Around

1. How are some animals today like the ancient dinosaurs?

   _____

2. What do animals need to survive?

   _____

3. Why do animals need their habitats?

   _____

4. What danger is there for some animals?

   _____

B. What can people do to help? Write.

_____

_____

_____

Writing

Explanatory Paragraph

In an explanatory paragraph, you can talk about **cause** and **effect** or result. When you talk about a cause, you tell why something happens or happened. When you talk about an effect or result, you explain what makes or made something happen. You can use words such as *so* and *because*.

- Use *so* to connect two sentences to show an effect or result. The first sentence shows the *cause* for something, and the second sentence shows the *effect* or result. Use a comma before *so*.
  People are cutting down bamboo forests. **+** The giant panda is in trouble. **=**
  People are cutting down bamboo forests, **so** the giant panda is in trouble.

- Use *because* to connect two sentences to show *why.* The first sentence shows the *effect* or *result,* and the second sentence shows the *cause*.
  The giant panda is in trouble. **+** People are cutting down bamboo forests. **=**
  The giant panda is in trouble **because** people are cutting down bamboo forests.

The Giant Panda Is in Danger
by Carol Barysh

The giant panda, the world's favorite black and white bear with the friendly face, is endangered for several reasons. One important reason is the panda's diet. About 99% of the panda's diet is bamboo. This key food is disappearing **because** people are cutting down the bamboo forests. A second reason has to do with its habitat. The wild giant panda lives only in parts of China, **so** there isn't enough space for a large panda population. In addition, the panda doesn't like to be around people and their activities. The panda's habitat is getting smaller **because** people are moving into the panda's space. Another reason is the short breeding season. Male and female pandas mate only from March to May, **so** not many baby pandas are born. And even when a mother panda has two new babies, she usually takes care of only one. For all these reasons, the giant panda is in danger.

Writing Assignment

Using the following steps, you will write a paragraph about an extinct or endangered animal. Be sure to explain why the animal died out or why it is endangered. Remember to use *so* and *because* when you talk about cause and effect.

13 Brainstorm ideas.

- Think of an extinct animal. Why did it die out?
- Think of an endangered animal. Why is it in trouble?

14 Use a cause & effect chart.

A cause & effect chart can help you organize your ideas.

The Giant Panda Is in Danger		
Cause	→	**Effect or Result**
People are cutting down bamboo forests.	→	The panda doesn't have enough food.
The panda lives only in parts of China.	→	There isn't enough space for many pandas.
People are moving into the panda's habitat.	→	The panda's habitat is getting smaller.
The panda's breeding season is only 3 months.	→	Not many baby pandas are born.
Mother pandas take care of just one baby.	→	Some baby pandas don't survive.

Practice organizing ideas for your own explanatory paragraph.

Cause	→	**Effect or Result**
	→	
	→	
	→	
	→	
	→	

To help you...

Writing Tip: In your sentences, use *so* when the cause comes first.
Use *because* when the effect or result comes first.

15 Write.

Use your cause & effect chart to organize your explanatory paragraph. Write your
paragraph on a separate piece of paper.

Review

16 **Write questions or answers.**

I. What happened to the dinosaurs?

_____

2. How long did the dinosaurs live?

_____

3. _____

The Pyrenean ibex died out.

4. Why did the Pyrenean ibex die out?

_____

5. _____

The last ibex died in January 2000.

17 **Complete the note cards about the two endangered animals.**

Endangered animal: _The Giant Panda_

What is happening to the giant panda?

Why is this happening?

What can people do to help?

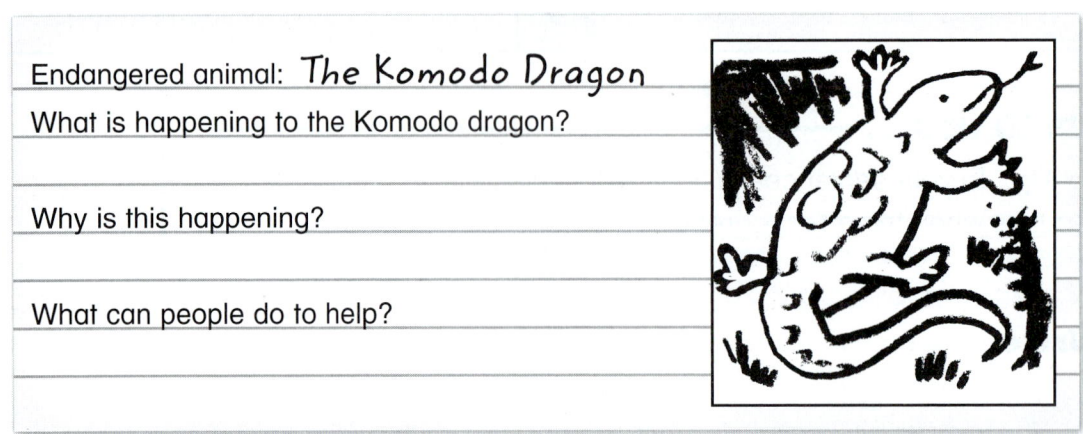

Endangered animal: _The Komodo Dragon_

What is happening to the Komodo dragon?

Why is this happening?

What can people do to help?

58

Communication Activity

Work with a partner: Student A uses this information and Student B turns to page 60.

Student A

A. Choose an extinct and an endangered animal. You can choose animals from the unit or other ones you like. Complete the chart.

B. Find a partner. Ask your partner questions. Listen and write the answers.

C. Answer your partner's questions.

Question	You	Your partner:
What *extinct* animal?	Steller's sea cow	Dodo bird
What happened to it?		
When did it die out?		
Where did it die out?		
What *endangered* animal?		
What is happening to it?		
Where does it live?		
What can people do to help?		

Students can choose extinct animals or endangered animals from the unit. If they chose other animals, encourage them to do research in the library or on the Internet.

Communication Activity

Work with a partner: Student B uses this information and Student A turns to page 59.

Student B

A. Choose an extinct and an endangered animal. You can choose animals from the unit or other ones you like. Complete the chart.

B. Work with your partner. Answer your partner's questions.

C. Ask your partner questions. Listen and write the answers.

Question	You	Your partner:
What *extinct* animal?	Dodo bird	Steller's sea cow
What happened to it?		
When did it die out?		
Where did it die out?		
What *endangered* animal?		
What is happening to it?		
Where does it live?		
What can people do to help?		

6 In the Old Days

1 **Listen and answer the questions.
Write complete sentences.**

Way Back Then

1. Was life faster or slower way back then?

   _____

2. Did people have telephones back then?

   _____

3. When people wanted to have a talk, what did they do?

   _____

4. When people went somewhere far, how did they travel?

   _____

5. When people read at night, what did they do?

   _____

How did people live long ago?

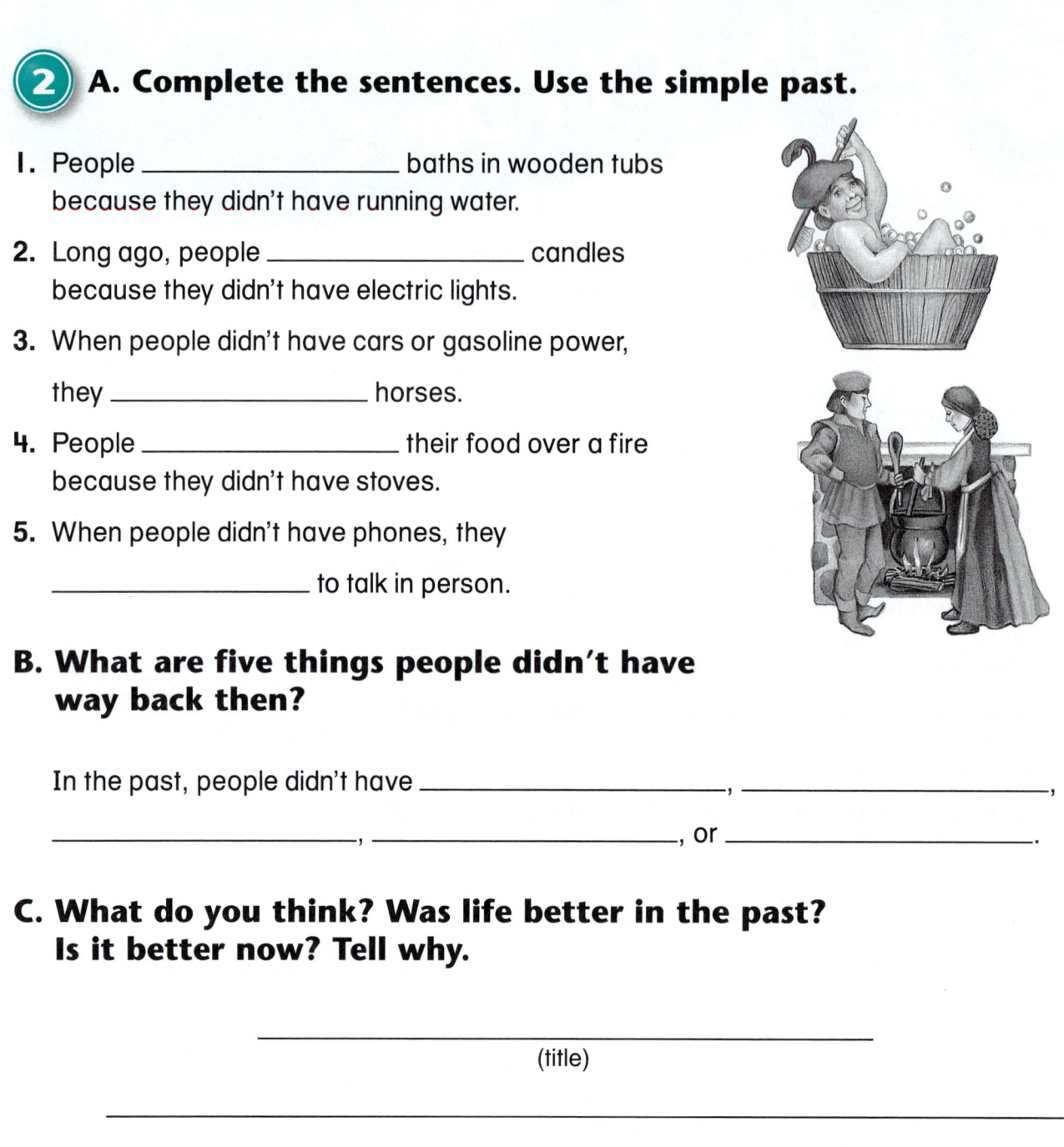

② A. Complete the sentences. Use the simple past.

1. People _____ baths in wooden tubs because they didn't have running water.

2. Long ago, people _____ candles because they didn't have electric lights.

3. When people didn't have cars or gasoline power,

   they _____ horses.

4. People _____ their food over a fire because they didn't have stoves.

5. When people didn't have phones, they

   _____ to talk in person.

B. What are five things people didn't have way back then?

In the past, people didn't have _____, _____,

_____, _____, or _____.

C. What do you think? Was life better in the past? Is it better now? Tell why.

_____
(title)

_____

_____

_____

_____

_____

_____

_____

_____

Grammar

Did people **travel** by car in the past?	No, they **didn't**. They **didn't have** cars then.
Did they **travel** by horse and carriage?	Yes, they **did**. They **had** carriages then.

3 **Write Yes, they did or No, they didn't.**

1. Did people travel by plane in the past?

   _____

2. Did people wash clothes by hand in the past?

   _____

3. Did they have CD players in the past?

   _____

4. Did people use computers in the past?

   _____

5. Did they burn candles in the past?

   _____

4 **What was school like in the past? Write complete sentences. Use the simple past.**

1. Students didn't have notebooks. They had slates to write on.

   have notebooks / have slates

2. _____

   ride buses / walk

3. _____

   sit at desks / sit on benches

4. _____

   use backpacks / use belts

5. _____

   have electric lights / burn candles

6. _____

   write with pens / write with chalk

Habit in the Past: **used to** + verb

How **did** people **use to travel**?

They **used to travel** by horse and carriage. Now they have cars.

Where **did** you **use to live**?

I **used to live** on Green Street. Now I live on Palm Avenue.

What musical instrument do you play?

I **used to play** the piano. Now I play the guitar.

5 **Complete the sentences. Write *use to* or *used to*.**

1. What did people _____ do before running water?

   They _____ wash in a wooden tub.

2. What did people _____ do before stoves?

   They _____ cook in an iron pot over a fire.

3. What did people _____ do before electric sewing machines?

   They _____ sew with a needle and thread.

4. What did people _____ do before they had money?

   They _____ use shells and beads instead of money.

6 **How is Ken's life different from before? Use the cues to write sentences.**

1. Ken used to play the flute. Now he plays the drums.

   then: flute / now: drums

2. _____

   then: one brother / now: new baby brother

   Ken

3. _____

   then: favorite subject math / now: favorite subject English

4. _____

   then: pet goldfish / now: pet parrot

5. _____

   then: soccer / now: basketball

7 **Answer the riddles. Write letters on the lines.**

[i]

1. Before me, people used to protect their wounds with sawdust. What am I?

___ ___ [ ] ___ ___ ___ ___

2. People used to cook in an iron pot over a fire, before me. What am I?

___ ___ ___ [ ] ___

3. People used to trade me for things they needed. What am I?

___ ___ [ ] ___ ___ ___

[n]

4. Students used to write on me before they had notebooks. What am I?

___ ___ ___ [ ] ___

[i]

5. People used to play me on an old gramophone. What am I?

___ ___ ___ [ ] ___ ___

6. In the past, people used to burn me for light. What am I?

___ ___ [ ] ___ ___ ___

What's the mystery word? ➝ [ ][ ][ ][ ][ ][ ][ ][ ][ ]

8 **How is your life different from when you were little? Write sentences.**

> I used to sleep with the light on. Now I sleep with the light off.

1. _____

2. _____

3. _____

4. _____

5. _____

Inventive Ideas: The Imagination Magazine

Read *Inventive Ideas: The Imagination Magazine*.

9 **Read. Check T for *True* and F for *False*.**

Do You Speak Doggish?

	T	F
1. A German company invented a machine that translates the barks of a dog.	☐	☐
2. This machine includes a microphone that goes on the dog's collar.	☐	☐

Our Readers Write Us

	T	F
3. Egyptian doctors used to make toothpaste from powdered stone and vinegar.	☐	☐
4. Joseph Merlin first invented ice skates and then roller skates.	☐	☐
5. Yo-yos used to be made from ivory and silk cord.	☐	☐
6. The yo-yo is a Philippine invention.	☐	☐

This Month's Contest Winner

10 **The magazine is having a new contest. Draw an invention and tell what it does.**

_____

_____

_____

_____

_____

_____

_____

_____

11 Listen and circle.

1. From ancient Sumerian tablets, we know that people used to mix together **ashes and fats**. / **water and salt**.

2. We **are sure** / **aren't sure** if Sumerians used to clean their clothes and bodies with these mixtures.

3. In ancient Greece and Rome, people used to wash clothes with different combinations of **plants, clays, and potash**. / **olive oil and vinegar**.

4. Ancient Romans used to oil their bodies and then clean off the dirty oil with **sheets of papyrus**. / **a special instrument**.

5. Soap as we know it was a common product in the **sixteenth century**. / **eighteenth century**.

12 A. Listen. Write numbers to show the order of events.

Tell Us, Grandpa

B. Imagine you are a grandparent. Tell what you used to do.

When I was your age, I _____

_____

Writing

Descriptive Paragraph

In a descriptive paragraph, you try to create a clear picture of a person, place, thing, or activity. Details help your reader "see" or imagine what the person, place, thing, or activity is like. A good description makes the reader feel as if he or she is actually there.

> **Before Fire**
> by Marina Lipska
>
> Before human beings learned to control fire thousands of years ago, life for a human family was very hard. Usually, a group of people lived together in a cave. Their basic activities depended on daytime and nighttime. During the day, they would look for food. Some of the women and children looked for berries and plants to eat. Some of the men hunted animals for meat. Before fire, cave people used to eat their meat raw and bloody, without cooking it. They had to eat everything quickly, before the meat started to smell. In the light of day, some of the people made clothes for themselves and for others from plant material and animal skins. Some used stones to make simple weapons. But at night, without fire, things were different. The people had to stay in their dark cave to protect themselves from animal attacks and from cold weather. In the dark, they couldn't make clothes or weapons. They couldn't hunt. They tried to sleep through the cold, and hoped the sun would rise to help them get warm the next day. Before fire, their lives were very hard.

Writing Assignment

Using the following steps, you will write a descriptive paragraph about a time in the past.

 Brainstorm ideas.

- Think of different times in history. Which time do you want to write about?
- What was life like back then? Think of details.

 Use an idea map.

An idea map can help you organize details. Write the main idea of your paragraph in the center. Write details in the boxes around the center. Use a different box for each detail you add.

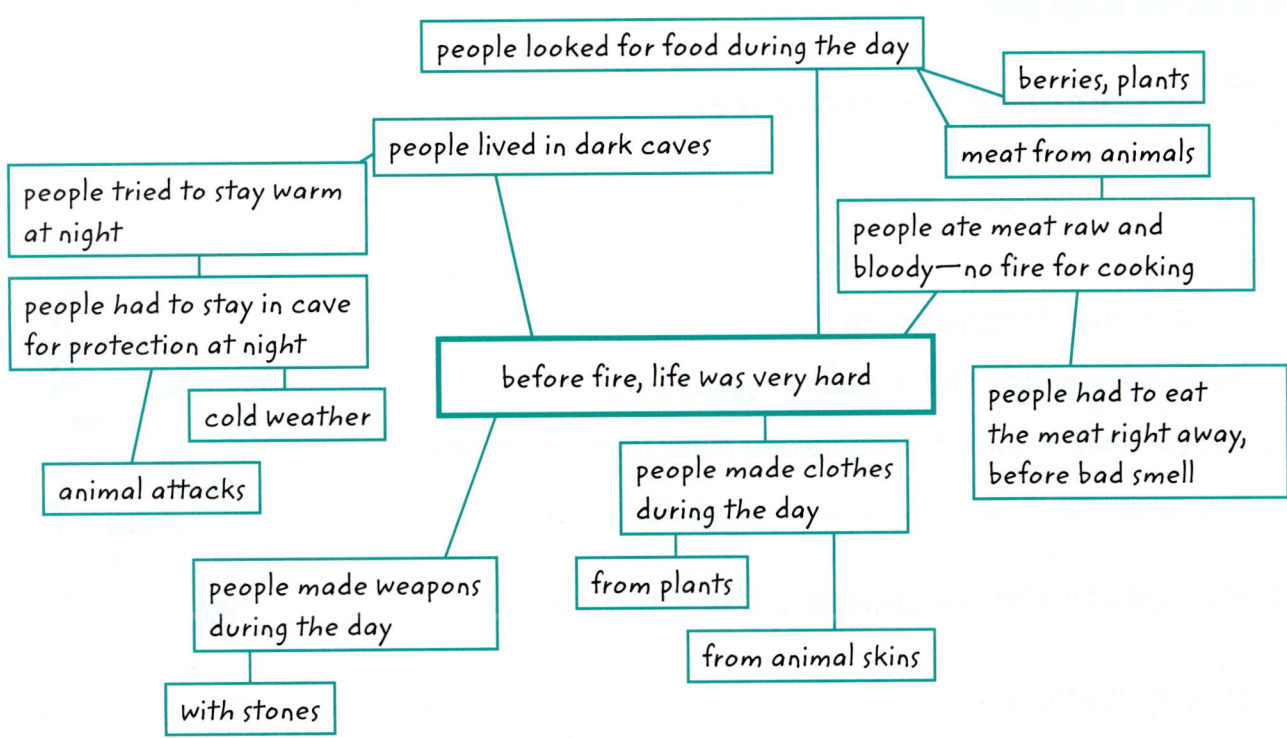

Now complete the idea map about your topic. Add a square for each detail.

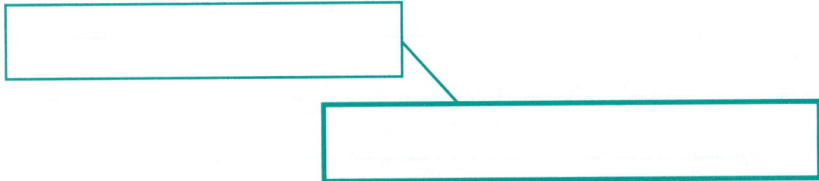

 **Write.**

Use your idea map to help you organize the details you listed for your descriptive paragraph. Write your paragraph on a separate piece of paper.

Review

16 **A. Complete the sentences.**

1. In the old days, people took baths in wooden tubs because they didn't

   have _____ .

2. To read, they used light from a _____

   because they didn't have electric lights.

3. People used to listen to singers and musicians in person because

   they didn't have _____ .

B. Complete the sentences. Use _used to_.

1. Before stoves, people _____

   _____ .

2. Before CDs, people _____

   _____ .

3. Before notebooks, students _____

   _____ .

4. Before cars, people _____

   _____ .

17 **Complete the questions and then write answers.**
Use _did/use to_ or _used to_.

1. In the old days, _____ people _____ have

   bandages? No, they didn't. They _____ use sawdust or spider webs.

2. A long time ago, _____ people _____ have phones?

   No, they didn't. They _____ talk in person.

3. When you were a baby, _____ you _____ cry?

   _____

Communication Activity

A. Cut out the cards.

B. Find a partner. Mix your cards together and put them facedown.

C. Before you take a card, say *In the old days* or *Now*. Then pick a card. Make two complete sentences with *In the old days* or *Now* and the word(s) on the card.

D. Give yourself one point for each correct sentence you make. Take turns.

E. The person with the most points is the winner.

> **In the old days people didn't have phones. They had to speak to each other in person.**

> **Good job! You used two correct sentences. You get two points.**

phones	carriages	candles	running water
stoves	horses	paper money	records
bandages	slates	buses	toothpaste

It's a Date!

1 **A. Listen. Check T for *True* and F for *False*.**

Special Days

	T	F
1. In France, New Year's Day is January first.	☐	☐
2. In Iran, New Year's Day is March first.	☐	☐
3. In India, Mother's Day is in November.	☐	☐
4. In Portugal, Mother's Day is in May.	☐	☐
5. Some countries celebrate Independence Day.	☐	☐
6. There is a birthday party with presents today.	☐	☐

B. Answer the questions.

1. In your country, when do you celebrate the New Year?

   _____

2. When do you celebrate Mother's Day?

   _____

3. Do you celebrate Independence Day? If so, when?

   _____

4. When do you celebrate your birthday?

   _____

What's your special day?

2 **Look at Betsy's agenda for last week. Then complete the paragraph.**

Monday, October 7	Dad's birthday
Tuesday, October 8	math test
Wednesday, October 9	piano lesson
Thursday, October 10	soccer practice
Friday, October 11	movie with Karen and Jill
Saturday, October 12	shopping with Aunt Laura
Sunday, October 13	clean my room

Last week, Betsy was a busy girl. On <u>Monday, October seventh</u>,
she and her mother had a birthday party for her dad. She helped her mother make
the cake and wrap the presents. On _____,
Betsy had a big math test. She studied hard and did well on the test. On
_____, she had her weekly piano lesson
after school. On _____, Betsy went to soccer
practice. This is her second year on the soccer team. She really enjoys soccer.
On _____, Betsy went to the movies with her
friends. They had a good time. On _____, she
went shopping with Aunt Laura. Betsy's aunt bought her some school clothes. On
_____, Betsy got up late. Then, after breakfast,
she cleaned her room. She made her bed, dusted, and swept the floor.

Future plans: *be* + *going to* + verb

When **are** you **going to visit** your grandmother?
   I'**m going to visit** her next week.
When is he **going to see** the fireworks?
   He'**s going to see** the fireworks at 9:30 P.M.
Mr. Martin, when **are** we **going to have** our math test?
   You'**re going to have** it on Thursday.

3 **Complete the sentences. Use *going to* and the verb.**

1. When _____ Gina _____ (get)
   her new bike?

2. We _____ (play) basketball this afternoon
   at 4:00.

3. I _____ (write) my cousin a letter tonight.

4. Why _____ you _____ (throw)
   that notebook away?

5. Lucy and Bill _____ (see) the parade
   tomorrow.

4 **Look at the pictures. Write sentences with *going to*.**

Angela

Tom and Bob

Grace and you

Dimitri

1. _____

2. _____

3. _____

4. _____

Look at the calendar. Answer each question with a complete sentence.

May 1	2	3	4
Ann's soccer game	Dan's dentist appointment	Nancy's class trip to the zoo	Greg's birthday party

1. What are Ann's parents going to do on the first?

   _____

2. Who is Dan going to see on the second?

   _____

3. Where is Nancy's class going to go on the third?

   _____

4. When is Greg going to have a birthday party?

   _____

6 **A. Write the dates for Saturday and Sunday. Then write your plans for the weekend.**

May 1	2
Friday, the first	chess club 4:00 dinner at Aunt Sally's house 8:00
Saturday	
Sunday	

B. Work with a partner. Ask about his or her plans. Write complete sentences.

1. On Saturday, _____

   _____.

2. On Sunday, _____

   _____.

7 **A. Read the clues. Write the letters of each word in the squares.**

1. In Thailand, people celebrate this festival of light.

2. In India, people celebrate this day in the Hindu month of Kartika.

3. In Sweden, people honor Saint Lucia in this month.

4. In China, people celebrate a festival with this.

5. In Portugal, people honor their mothers in this month.

B. Use the letters in the blue squares above to make a word that completes the question below.

What is your favorite __ __ __ __ __ __ __?

C. Now answer the question and tell why.

My favorite _____

_____.

8 **Jack has a big problem. What do you think he is going to do?**

_____

_____

_____

_____

_____

_____

_____

_____

Day by Day: The Magazine that Celebrates Every Day

Read *Day by Day: The Magazine that Celebrates Every Day.*

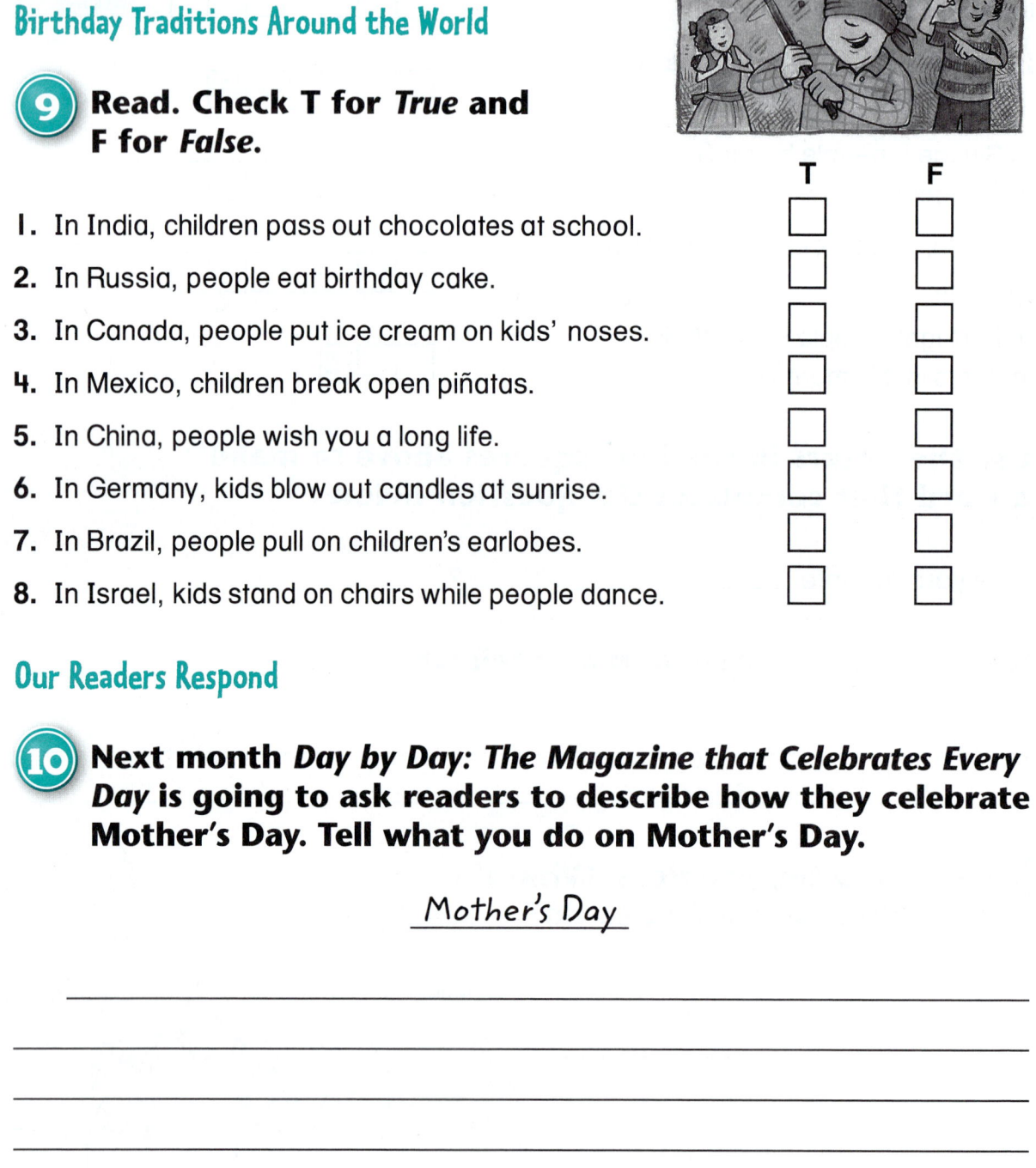

Birthday Traditions Around the World

9 **Read. Check T for *True* and F for *False*.**

	T	F
1. In India, children pass out chocolates at school.	☐	☐
2. In Russia, people eat birthday cake.	☐	☐
3. In Canada, people put ice cream on kids' noses.	☐	☐
4. In Mexico, children break open piñatas.	☐	☐
5. In China, people wish you a long life.	☐	☐
6. In Germany, kids blow out candles at sunrise.	☐	☐
7. In Brazil, people pull on children's earlobes.	☐	☐
8. In Israel, kids stand on chairs while people dance.	☐	☐

Our Readers Respond

10 **Next month *Day by Day: The Magazine that Celebrates Every Day* is going to ask readers to describe how they celebrate Mother's Day. Tell what you do on Mother's Day.**

Mother's Day

_____

_____

_____

_____

_____

_____

_____

11 Listen. What is going to happen? Write sentences with *going to.*

1. She _____ .

2. He _____ .

3. She _____ .

4. She _____ .

5. He _____ .

12 Write rhyming words on the lines. Listen to check.

Earth Day

Next week Earth Day is coming.

What are you going to _____?

We're going to plant some flowers.

You could help us, _____!

We're going to clean the playground

    and pick up trash on the _____.

We're listing things to recycle,

    and then we'll give a _____.

We're decorating grocery bags

    and bringing them to a _____.

They'll give the bags to customers,

    who'll use the bags some _____.

We're having a fair on Earth Day,

    so everybody can take _____.

We're going to help our planet.

Don't you think that's _____?

beach	do
more	part
smart	speech
store	too

Writing

Paragraph Unity

The topic sentence tells the main idea of your paragraph. Your detail sentences give facts and examples about the main idea. Your paragraph has unity when *all* of the detail sentences relate to the main idea. After you write a paragraph, look for sentences that don't belong and take them out.

La Tomatina
by Manolo Hurtado

My favorite holiday is the big tomato fight called "La Tomatina" in my town of Buñol, Spain. Every year on the last Wednesday in August, many trucks full of red, ripe tomatoes come into the center of town. ~~My uncle bought a truck last year.~~ Everyone who wants to be part of the tomato fight is waiting in the streets. At exactly 11:00 A.M., everyone grabs tomatoes and the throwing begins. The tomatoes are very soft, and they smash against the people, buildings, cars, and streets. ~~Tomatoes are very good for you because they have a lot of vitamins.~~ In just minutes, the town and everyone in it is bright red. In fact, it looks like it rained tomato juice instead of water! The tomato throwing, running, hiding, rolling around in tomatoes, and laughing lasts until 1:00 P.M. ~~Some people think the fight should stop at 12:00 noon.~~ Then the fight is officially over, and all the tired but happy, bright red people start the very big job of cleaning up the mess.

Look at the sentences below. The first sentence is the topic sentence of a paragraph. The sentences with numbers are detail sentences. Circle the number of each detail sentence that does *not* belong in the paragraph.

To welcome the New Year, Chinese families follow certain traditions.

1. Each family cleans its house from top to bottom to sweep away bad luck.

2. Family members decorate their doors and windows with bright colors and symbols of long life, wealth, and happiness.

3. Many Chinese houses are in the pagoda style.

4. The night before the New Year begins, families eat a delicious meal of seafood, dumplings, and other foods that symbolize good luck and prosperity.

5. I don't like seafood, but I like dumplings a lot.

6. The celebration continues with singing and dancing, and a colorful parade with a big dragon that dances and weaves through the streets.

Writing Assignment

Using the following steps, you will write a paragraph about a holiday, special day, or event that you enjoy or celebrate.

 **Brainstorm ideas.**

- Choose a holiday, special day, or event.
- When is it celebrated?
- How long does the holiday or event last?
- How is it celebrated? What do people do?

 Use a list.

After you decide on a topic sentence, make a list of details you could include in your paragraph. Then go back and look at each detail carefully. If a detail doesn't relate directly to the topic sentence, cross it off your list.

_____
(topic sentence)

1. _____

2. _____

3. _____

4. _____

5. _____

6. _____

7. _____

8. _____

 Write.

Use your list of details to help you organize your detail sentences. Then write your paragraph on a separate piece of paper.

— To help you... —

Editing Tip: Show your paragraph to a friend. Can he or she find any sentences that don't belong? Make changes if necessary.

Review

16 **Write words.**

June	June	June	June	June	June
1	2	3	4	16	20

first _____ _____ _____ _____ _____

17 **Answer the questions. Use *going to*.**

1. In France, what are they going to do on January first?

   _____

2. In India, what are they going to do on Diwali?

   _____

3. In China, what are they going to do on the fifteenth day of the New Year?

   _____

4. In Sweden, what are they going to do on Saint Lucia's Day?

   _____

5. In Thailand, what are they going to do for Loi Krathong?

   _____

18 **Use the cues to write questions. Use *going to*.**

1. _____

   José / have / birthday party / May 24

2. _____

   William and Sally / see / parade

3. _____

   you / play / baseball / 4:00 P.M.

4. _____

   school / start again / January 7

19 **What are you going to do on your next birthday? Write.**

_____

Communication Activity

Work with a partner: Student A uses this information and Student B turns to page 84.

A. Look at Sam's calendar. Ask what Sam is going to do on the dates with a question mark (?). Write the answers.

B. Then answer your partner's questions.

What is Sam going to do on the second?

He's going to go shopping.

Sam's July Schedule

Sunday	Monday	Tuesday	Wednesday	Thursday	Friday	Saturday
1 soccer	2 ? *shopping*	3 plant trees	4 ?	5 dentist	6	7
8 ?	9	10	11	12	13	14
15 birthday party	16 ?	17	18	19	20 watch full moon	21
22	23	24	25 ?	26	27	28
29	30	31				

Communication Activity

Work with a partner: Student B uses this information and Student A turns to page 83.

A. Look at Sam's calendar.
Answer your partner's questions.

B. Then ask what Sam is going to do on the dates with a question mark (?). Write the answers.

What is Sam going to do on the second?

He's going to go shopping.

Sam's July Schedule

Sunday	Monday	Tuesday	Wednesday	Thursday	Friday	Saturday
1 ?	2 shopping	3 ?	4 fireworks	5 ?	6	7
8 lunch with Sara	9	10	11	12	13	14
15 ?	16 march in a parade	17	18	19	20 ?	21
22	23	24	25 doctor	26	27	28
29	30	31				

8 Hobbies Are Fun!

1 Write words that rhyme on the lines.
Then listen to check your answers.

Hobbies

better	clocks
do	everyone
fun	kite
letter	night
rocks	you

It's exciting to have a hobby.

Hobbies are lots of _____.

You can take photos or build model planes.

There are hobbies for _____.

Some people draw or paint.

Some watch stars at _____.

Others make jewelry or sew their clothes.

You can even make and fly your own _____.

It's fun to look for and fun to trade

cards, shells, or _____.

You never know what you will find.

Some people like to fix old _____.

Collections of marbles are good,

but comic books are _____.

Collecting stamps is always the best

if you need to mail a _____.

It's such fun to have a hobby.

There's a perfect one for _____.

Try some interesting new ones.

You'll find what you like to _____.

2 Read. Then answer the questions.

Allen: Look! The Arts & Crafts Store is having a sale. Let's go in.

Erica: OK. I used to have a hobby. Maybe it's time to find a new one.

Mary: It's fun to try out new hobbies. Look, all the things you need to make jewelry are 50% off!

Erica: The price is cheap, but I think making jewelry is kind of boring.

Allen: Well, how about coin collecting? It's fun to learn where coins came from and how old they are.

Erica: My brother collects coins. I want to try something different.

Mary: I think it's exciting to draw and paint. And watercolor paints are on sale!

Erica: I don't draw well. What else is here?

Allen: Look over here. There are model kits of all kinds. I think building models is great.

Erica: I don't want to build little cars, trains, or planes! Yuck.

Mary: Well, let's go.

Erica: Wait! Look! I see balls of yarn over there, and knitting needles. I think it's cool to make your own scarves and sweaters.

Allen: You do? Then knitting can be your hobby!

1. What does Mary think about new hobbies?

_____

2. Why doesn't Erica want to make jewelry?

_____

3. Why does Allen like coin collecting?

_____

4. What does Mary think about painting?

_____

5. Who likes building models?

_____

6. What hobby does Erica decide to try? Why?

_____

Ella's building is **tall**.
Sandy's building is **taller than** Ella's building.
Chris's building is the **tallest** of all.

| comparing two things: | tall**er than** |
| comparing three or more things: | **the tallest** of all |

3 **Write the -*er* and -*est* forms of the adjectives.**

	comparative: -*er/-r*	superlative: -*est/-st*
1. small	_____	_____
2. hard	_____	_____
3. big	_____	_____
4. pretty	_____	_____
5. nice	_____	_____
6. cheap	_____	_____

4 **Complete the sentences. Use -*er* + *than* or *the* + -*est*.**

1. My soccer card collection is _____ (small) Eddie's collection.

2. Bill thinks building models is _____ (great) hobby of all.

3. Erica thinks knitting is _____ (cool) hobby there is.

4. Kevin has _____ (big) comic book collection in our school.

5. Janet's bead necklace is _____ (short) Pam's necklace.

5 **Write a sentence about each scarf.**
Use *long*, *longer*, and *longest*.

1. _____

_____

2. _____

_____

3. _____

_____

| Moira | Kim | Jane |

6 **Look at the pictures. Complete the sentences. Use forms of _good_ in 1. and _bad_ in 2.**

1. Lois's cookies are _____. Jeff's chicken and

   vegetables are _____ the cookies. Peggy's soup

   is _____ of all.

2. Roger's singing is _____. Amanda's singing is

   _____ Roger's singing. Phil's singing is

   _____ of the three!

3. How is your singing? _____

   _____

7 **A. Make lists. Write three examples for each category.**

Singers	Sports Stars	Actors
• _____	• _____	• _____
• _____	• _____	• _____
• _____	• _____	• _____

B. Who is the best? Who is the worst? Write sentences for each category.

Singers: _____

_____

Sports Stars: _____

_____

Actors: _____

_____

8 **Find and circle eight words related to hobbies.**

```
C  B  M  A  R  B  L  E  S  O
O  C  H  E  E  B  A  H  F  F
I  D  O  J  A  C  A  R  D  S
N  E  B  C  P  H  R  O  L  T
S  F  A  V  A  E  D  C  W  A
R  G  G  I  G  S  X  K  K  M
S  H  E  L  L  S  M  S  S  P
H  I  L  M  E  R  N  O  C  S
U  K  N  I  T  T  I  N  G  Q
V  J  W  O  N  K  A  V  A  T
```

cards	chess
coins	knitting
marbles	rocks
shells	stamps

Read *Hobby Hour: The Magazine for Hours of Fun.*

⑨ Read. Check T for *True* and F for *False*.

Domino Topples

	T	F
1. You can do domino topples alone or with friends.	☐	☐
2. In domino topples, you see who can build the tallest tower of dominoes.	☐	☐
3. Domino topples are popular all over the world.	☐	☐
4. Scott Suko teaches children how to set up the longest and hardest domino designs.	☐	☐

World's Craziest Collections

5. Louise Greenfarb has the largest refrigerator magnet collection.	☐	☐
6. Jean F. Vernetti of Switzerland has "Do Not Disturb" signs from 2,915 countries.	☐	☐
7. The world's longest gum-wrapper chain is very heavy.	☐	☐

⑩ What do you think? Choose something you think would be fun to collect and tell why.

bottle caps	butterflies	cards
old records	Olympic pins	postcards
rubber bands	sports cards	stop signs

_____

_____

_____

_____

_____

_____

11 **Listen. Complete the chart.**

	Hobby	Opinion
Anita	sewing clothes for dolls	It's harder, because the clothes are smaller.
Luke		
Jane		
Charlie		
Linda		

12 **A. Listen to the chant. Check T for *True* and F for *False*.**

My Collections

		T	F
1.	This collector keeps some things in boxes.	☐	☐
2.	When he needs more space, he puts things under the bed.	☐	☐
3.	His boxes are very full, so he can't find things.	☐	☐
4.	He doesn't have enough comic books in his collection.	☐	☐
5.	He collects a lot of marbles.	☐	☐

B. What should this person do? Give some advice.

_____

_____

_____

_____

_____

Writing

Descriptive Paragraph: Object

When you describe an object, you use words that help your reader "see" what you are describing. You can use words that relate to the five senses—sight, sound, taste, smell, and touch. Using these words in your detail sentences builds a picture.

Look at the kinds of words this writer uses. She uses words that refer to four of the five senses. Which sense is *not* referred to in her paragraph?

> **My Favorite Music Box**
> by Mei-ling Chen
>
> I like each of the twenty music boxes in my collection, but my new favorite is a hand-carved wooden music box my father gave me. He bought it on a trip he took to Austria last month. On top of the round base is a tiny, perfect model of an old-fashioned wooden house. Around the house, there are four dark green trees with snow on their branches. The house itself has a tall, triangle-shaped roof. There is a bumpy chimney made of stone on the roof. It looks so real you can almost smell the smoke! The front door of the house has an arch at the top, and it is painted red. The four windows also have arches. There are small red-and-green checked curtains at the windows. By the front door, there is a boy. He is playing with his dog, who is jumping up to catch a stick. I love to wind the box up. Then the scene spins around and the colors blend together. As the box slows down, you see all the details. And you hear the tune "My Favorite Things" the whole time. This music box is one of my very favorite things! I really love my music box souvenir from Austria.

Write the words in the correct column. Some words can go in more than one column.

bumpy	delicious	fresh	happy	hard	heavy	loud	metal
purple	rough	round	salty	smooth	soft	sweet	tiny

sight	sound	taste	smell	touch

Writing Assignment

Using the following steps, you will write a descriptive paragraph about an object. Be sure to use words that help the reader form a picture of the object you describe.

 **Brainstorm ideas.**

- Choose an object from your classroom or from your home.
- What details can you describe?
- What words that relate to the senses can you use?

 **Use a 5-senses chart.**

Think of descriptive words you can use to write about your object. Which of the five senses do they refer to? Write your descriptive words in the correct column of the chart.

sight	sound	taste	smell	touch

┌─ To help you... ──────────────────────────

Writing Tip: You can describe your object's shape, size, cost, color, origin, materials, texture, weight, height, beauty, and purpose.

15 Write.

Use your 5-senses chart to help you organize your ideas. Write your descriptive paragraph on a separate piece of paper.

Review

16 **Look at the pictures. Name each hobby and tell what you think of it. Use words from the box.**

  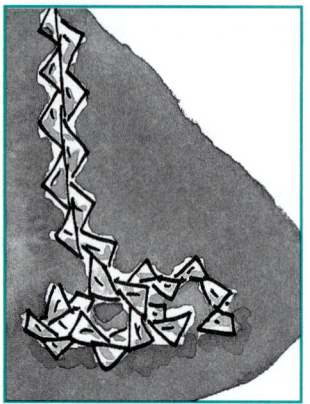 

| boring | cool | exciting | hard | interesting | silly |

1. _____

2. _____

3. _____

4. _____

17 **Read. Write a complete sentence to answer each question.**

1. Ray has a larger coin collection than Dan. Sue's coin collection is larger than Ray's.
Who has the largest coin collection of all?

_____

2. Liz has a better stamp collection than Ralph. Hector's stamp collection is worse than Ralph's.
Who has the best stamp collection?

_____

Who has the worst stamp collection?

_____

3. What's your hobby? Why do you like it?

_____

Communication Activity

A. Cut out the cards.

B. Find a partner. Mix your cards together and put them facedown.

C. Pick a card. Follow the instruction on the card. Use a complete sentence.

D. Get one point for each correct sentence you make. Take turns.

E. The person with the most points is the winner.

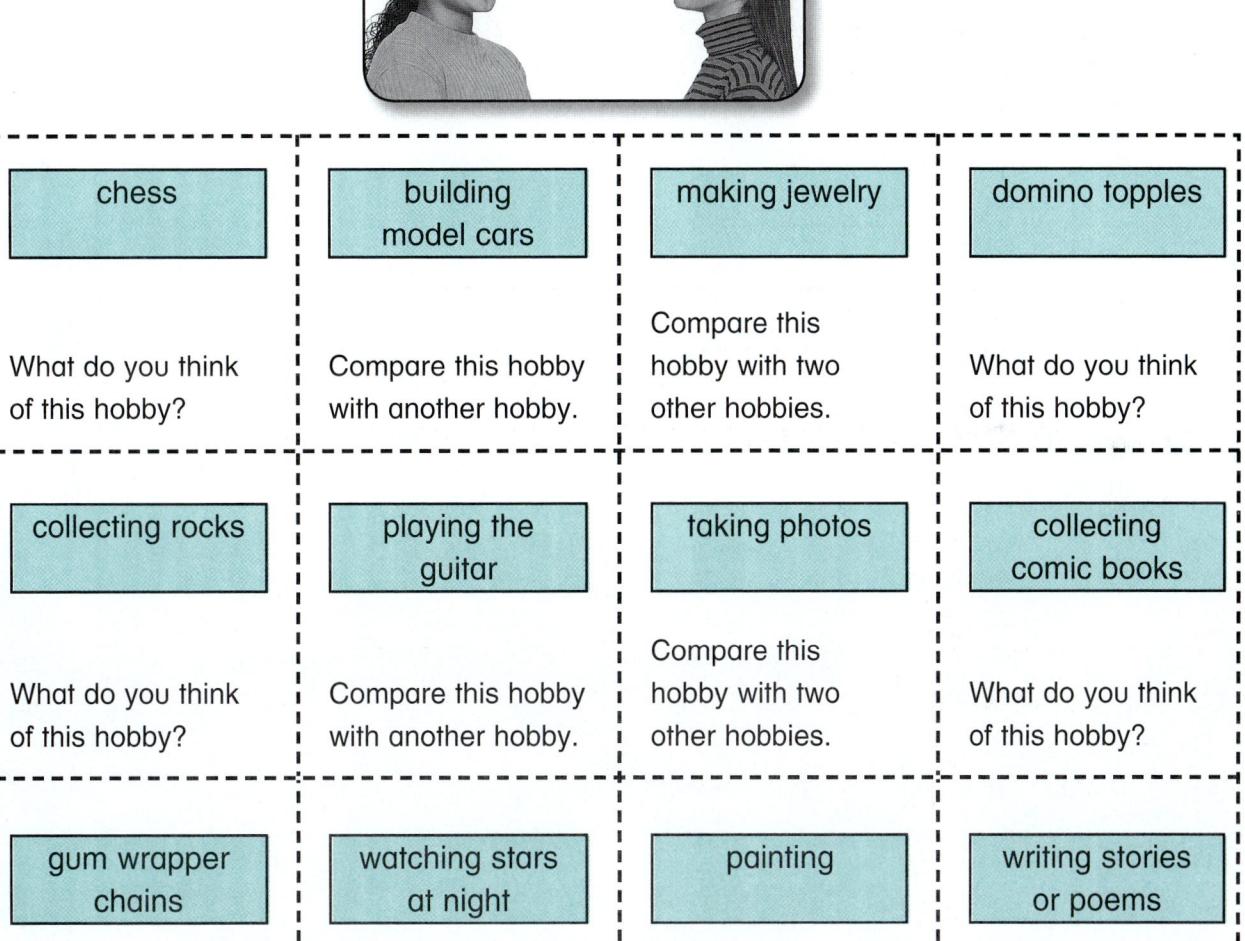

I think chess is very hard.

Good job! Your sentence is correct. You get one point.

chess	building model cars	making jewelry	domino topples
What do you think of this hobby?	Compare this hobby with another hobby.	Compare this hobby with two other hobbies.	What do you think of this hobby?
collecting rocks	playing the guitar	taking photos	collecting comic books
What do you think of this hobby?	Compare this hobby with another hobby.	Compare this hobby with two other hobbies.	What do you think of this hobby?
gum wrapper chains	watching stars at night	painting	writing stories or poems
What do you think of this hobby?	Compare this hobby with another hobby.	Compare this hobby with two other hobbies.	What do you think of this hobby?

Let's Dance!

TRACK 27

1 **Listen. Write the missing words. Then listen to check your answers.**

Dance Lessons

Welcome to our dance school.

What would you like to learn?

You could take _____,

  and stamp and clap and turn.

You could learn the _____,

  and maybe do the _____.

Would you like to _____?

You can. It's on our list!

Come take a chance!
We're going to teach you how to dance.
Footwork, arms, and stance!
We're going to teach you how to dance.

We have _____ lessons.

You can _____ and swing.

_____ is very popular,

  and _____ is quite the thing.

Many people learn to _____,

  others learn to _____.

But perhaps you would prefer

  to learn _____ or _____.

(Chorus)

ballet	flamenco
jazz	mambo
polka	rock and roll
salsa	samba
swing	tango
tap	waltz

Do you like to dance?

2 Write questions.

1. _____

Thanks. I'd love to disco dance!

2. _____

I'd like to learn how to swing dance.

3. _____

Yes, I'd like to learn how to do those steps.

4. _____

No, thanks. I can't dance fast.

5. _____

OK. But I'd need to have a partner, right?

3 How about you? Write your own answers.

1. What dance would you like to learn?

_____

_____

_____

2. Why would you like to learn that dance?

_____

_____

_____

3. Would you like to do a fast dance?

_____

_____

_____

4. Would you like to do a slow dance?

_____

_____

_____

Grammar

What does she **think of** the polka? She **thinks** the polka is lively.
What do you **think of** polka dancing? I **think** it's too hard.

4 **Write questions and answers. Use the words in ( ).**

1. Eric: _____? (the tango)

   Wanda: _____. (old-fashioned)

2. Scott _____? (the waltz)

   Sally: _____. (beautiful)

3. Maria: _____? (the jitterbug)

   Tim: _____. (too fast)

5 **Answer each question with a complete sentence.**

	jazz dancing	swing dancing	hat dancing	tap dancing
Kim and Pat	cool	old-fashioned	fun	exciting
Martha	too hard	easy	noisy	lively
Steve	too fast	graceful	neat	energetic

1. What does Steve think of jazz dancing?

   _____

2. What do Kim and Pat think of hat dancing?

   _____

3. What does Martha think of swing dancing?

   _____

4. What does Steve think of tap dancing?

   _____

5. What do Kim and Pat think of jazz dancing?

   _____

6. What does Martha think of hat dancing?

   _____

| Would | you they | like to learn how to flamenco dance? | Yes, No, | I they | would. wouldn't. |
| Would | he she | like to learn how to flamenco dance? | Yes, No, | he she | would. wouldn't. |

6 **Complete the chart. Write sentences to answer the questions.**

Dance School Classes

Name	disco dance	salsa dance	ballet dance	square dance
Jim	yes	yes	no	yes
Jane and Jill	yes	yes	yes	no
Susan	no	yes	yes	yes
You				

1. Would Jim like to learn how to ballet dance?

   _____

2. Would Jane and Jill like to learn how to salsa dance?

   _____

3. Would Susan like to learn how to disco dance?

   _____

4. Would you like to learn how to square dance?

   _____

5. Would Jim like to learn how to salsa dance?

   _____

6. Would Jane and Jill like to learn how to square dance?

   _____

7. Would you like to learn how to disco dance?

   _____

7 **Unscramble the dance steps and moves. Write the words.**

1. pastm   __ __ __ __ ⃝

2. pans greinfs   __ __ __ __ __   __ __ __ __ __ __ __ ⃝

3. pcal   __ __ ⃝ __

4. ikck   __ ⃝ __ __

5. untr   __ __ __ ⃝

6. veaw   __ __ __ ⃝

7. noij shdan   j __ __ __   (h) __ __ __ __

Write the circled letters below. Unscramble them to answer the question.

__ __ __ __ __ __ __

....
: How will doing any dance help you? : ➔ It will keep you ☐☐   ☐☐☐☐☐
....

8 **Ask four classmates. Write. Tell the class.**

What do you think of line dancing?

I think it's fun!

Name	line dancing	hip-hop	ballet	salsa
Jeremy	fun	lively	graceful	exciting
1.				
2.				
3.				
4.				

Read *Let's Dance Magazine*.

**** **Answer the questions.**

Rising Star

1. What does Brittany McAfee think of ballet dancing?

   _____

2. How does ballet dancing make her feel?

   _____

Dances Around the World

3. Would you like to watch a rain dance? Why?

   _____

Ballroom Dancing Is Popular Again

4. What do you think of ballroom dancing?

   _____

5. Would you like to learn the fox-trot? Why?

   _____

10 **Write to *Let's Dance Magazine*. Choose a dance for *Dances Around the World*. Describe it. Draw or glue a picture.**

Dance: _____

Country: _____

Steps: _____

Music: _____

What people think of it: _____

_____

_____

Why it should be in *Let's Dance Magazine*: _____

_____

 **Listen. Check *yes* or *no*.**

TRACK 28

	yes	no
1. They're going to take dance lessons.	☐	☐
2. He thinks hip-hop looks a little dangerous.	☐	☐
3. Carlos really knows how to dance salsa.	☐	☐
4. He thinks line dancing is easy.	☐	☐
5. He doesn't know how to dance.	☐	☐

TRACK 29

12 A. Listen. Circle what the dancers are told to do.

Shake a Leg

1. Get up.	5. Paint the whole town red.
2. Get up out of that sofa.	6. Dance 'til the sun goes down.
3. Shake a hand.	7. Shake a leg.
4. Tap your feet.	8. Jump up in the air.

B. Make up your own dance. Write what the dancers should do.

Example: *Get down! Clap your hands!*

1. _____

2. _____

3. _____

4. _____

C. Work with a partner. Describe your dances. Do you like your dance or your partner's dance better? Why or why not?

Unit 9

103

Writing

Opinion Paragraph

In an opinion paragraph, you describe how you think or feel about something. Then you give good reasons to show why you think that way. You can use expressions such as *in my opinion* and *I think* to introduce your opinion.

> **Dancing Is for Everyone**
> by Jack Williams
>
> **In my opinion,** people make a big mistake when they say they don't want to learn to dance. There are several reasons everyone should learn to appreciate dance. First, there is some form of dancing in every culture. Each country has its traditional dances and its popular dances. People in a culture should know as much about that culture's dance as they would about its art or music. Second, dancing is a form of exercise. It develops muscles and raises the heartbeat, just as practicing a sport does. Good dancing requires control, balance, strength, and grace. These are all good qualities to have. Third, **I think** learning to dance builds confidence, and makes social events, such as parties, much more comfortable. A good dancer is always welcome at parties and is enjoyable to watch. And last but not least, dancing is a lot of fun. For these reasons, I think dancing is for everyone.

Read the paragraph again. Then list on the chart the four main reasons that support the writer's opinion.

There are several reasons everyone should learn to appreciate dance.
1.
2.
3.
4.

Writing Assignment

Using the following steps, you will write an opinion paragraph about a topic of your choice. Be sure to include at least three good reasons to support your opinion.

 **Brainstorm ideas.**

- Pick one of these topics or a topic of your own.
    - Everyone should play a musical instrument.
    - Everyone should practice a sport.
    - Everyone needs a hobby.
    - Video games are for teenagers, not children.
    - Reading comic books is a waste of time.
- What reasons can you think of to support your opinion?

 Use a chart.

Use a chart to list the reasons you have for your opinion. Write your topic sentence at the top and the reasons that support your opinion by the numbers.

1.	
2.	
3.	
4.	

┌─ **To help you...** ─────────────────────
| **Expressions:** |
| for these reasons   in my opinion   I think |
└────────────────────────────────────

 **Write.**

Use your chart to help you organize your detail sentences. Then write your opinion paragraph on a separate piece of paper.

Review

16 Complete the sentences.

1. Ellen: _____ you _____ to dance?

   Ed: No, thanks. _____ to take a break. Let's just watch!

2. Karen: _____ you _____ to do this line dance?

   Keith: Yes, _____. Let's get started!

17 Answer the questions.

1. Would you like to learn the samba?

   Yes, _____.

2. Would Paul like to waltz?

   No, _____.

3. Would they like to line dance?

   Yes, _____.

4. Would they like to do the polka?

   No, _____.

18 Write a question or an answer.

1. What do you think of the jitterbug?

   _____

2. _____

   Leslie thinks ballroom dancing is cool.

3. What do you think of swing dancing?

   _____

4. _____

   Sam thinks the twist is fun.

Communication Activity

Work with a partner: Student A uses this information and Student B turns to page 108.

Student A

A. Complete the chart.

B. Find a partner. Ask your partner questions. Listen and write the answers.

C. Answer your partner's questions.

What do you think of Mexican hat dancing?

I think it's fun.

What	You	Your partner
Mexican hat dancing	It's exciting.	It's fun.
disco dancing		
line dancing		
square dancing		
flamenco dancing		
salsa dancing		
fan dancing		
ballroom dancing		
tap dancing		
ballet dancing		
hip-hop		
jazz dancing		
folk dancing		
circle dancing		

Communication Activity

Work with a partner: Student B uses this information and Student A turns to page 107.

Student B

A. Complete the chart.

B. Find a partner. Answer your partner's questions.

C. Ask your partner questions. Listen and write the answers.

What do you think of Mexican hat dancing?

I think it's fun.

What	You	Your partner
Mexican hat dancing	It's fun.	It's exciting.
disco dancing		
line dancing		
square dancing		
flamenco dancing		
salsa dancing		
fan dancing		
ballroom dancing		
tap dancing		
ballet dancing		
hip-hop		
jazz dancing		
folk dancing		
circle dancing		

Grammar Handbook Practice

1 *Be:* Write the present and past forms of *be.*

Present of *be*

I _____ We _____

You _____ You _____

He/she/it _____ They _____

Past of *be*

I _____ We _____

You _____ You _____

He/she/it _____ They _____

2 *Be:* Write the present and past forms of *be.*

1. Where _____ you yesterday? I didn't see you at school.

2. Alicia _____ at the dentist's office today.

3 **Adjectives:** Write the comparative forms.

1. big _____
2. curly _____
3. friendly _____
4. long _____

5. pretty _____
6. sad _____
7. short _____
8. tall _____

4 **Adjectives:** Complete the sentences.

1. (old) Lydia is _____ than Darlene.

2. (straight) Ana's hair is _____ than Sally's hair.

3. (strong) Luis is _____ than Billy.

4. (slow) A turtle is _____ than a rabbit.

5 *Get:* Complete the sentences with *get* and an adjective.

1. (impatient) I _____ when the school bus is late.

2. (upset) Sonia _____ when she has a bad grade.

3. (excited) They _____ when our team wins the game.

4. (scared) My little sister _____ when she sees a spider.

Grammar Handbook Practice

1 **Present Progressive:** Check *now* or *later* for the meaning.

	now	later
1. Chris can't come to the phone. He's taking a shower.	☐	☐
2. I can't come. I'm going to the store with my mom at 5:00.	☐	☐

2 **Present Progressive referring to the Future:** Complete the sentences.

1. (do) What _____ you _____ this weekend?
2. (visit) I _____ _____ my grandmother.
3. (help) Sara _____ _____ her mom clean the house.
4. (play) Sam and Marco _____ _____ soccer at 3:30.
5. (shop) Lucy _____ _____ for a birthday present.

3 **Habit in the Present:** Complete the sentences.

1. (play) Soo-jin _____ chess in her free time.
2. (sing) Leo and his friends _____ in The Tones.
3. (work) I _____ in our garden in my free time.
4. (practice) We _____ the piano every day.

4 **Habit in the Present:** Unscramble the sentences.

1. twice/Linda/a/swimming/week/goes

   _____

2. Roberto/school/usually/drums/plays/the/after

   _____

3. cleans/Sonia/her/always/weekends/room/on

   _____

4. grandparents/year/three/my/visit/times/me/a

   _____

5. Sundays/have/we/on/park/a/the/picnic/in

   _____

Grammar Handbook Practice

1 *Like:* Is the meaning the same or different? Circle.

1. I like chicken. I want some chicken now.　　　**same / different**

2. I'll have a bowl of soup. I'd like a bowl of soup.　**same / different**

3. I'd like some ice cream. I like ice cream.　　　**same / different**

2 *Like:* Complete the conversation. Use *have*, *like*, and *want*.

Waiter:　What would you like?

Gloria:　I'd _____ a cheese sandwich and a soda.

Frank:　And I _____ a hamburger and fries.

Waiter:　Do you want something to drink?

Frank:　I'll _____ a glass of water.

3 **Count and Noncount Nouns:** Write *a*, *an*, *some*, or *any*.

1. I want _____ pizza.

2. I'd like _____ apple.

3. Sue wants _____ sandwich.

4. There's _____ book on the table.

5. There isn't _____ paper.

6. There are _____ pens in the desk.

4 *Would* + **Verb:** Write sentences with *would*.

1. (you/eat/fufu/?) _____

2. (I/try/bean/paste) _____

3. (Carmen/eat/sushi) _____

5 *Would* + **Verb:** Write sentences about you with *would* or *wouldn't*.

1. Would you eat colcannon from Ireland?

　_____

2. Would you jump off a bridge?

　_____

Grammar Handbook Practice

1 Reflexive Pronouns: Write the correct pronoun.

1. I wear sunscreen. I take care of _____.

2. Cathy doesn't wear her bike helmet. She could hurt _____.

3. They ate too much candy. They didn't control _____.

4. Be careful! You could fall and hurt _____!

5. We love swimming in the lake. We really enjoy _____.

6. Wear your soccer equipment, boys. Don't forget to protect _____.

2 Should + Verb: Write should or shouldn't.

1. I have an earache. What _____ I do?

2. I can't find my homework. What _____ I tell the teacher?

3. You _____ swim alone. It's dangerous.

4. When you are exercising, you _____ have a bottle of water with you.

5. You _____ stay up late. You need to get enough sleep.

6. Rick _____ study more. His grades aren't very good.

3 Should + Verb: Write complete sentences.

1. Your friend Pat doesn't understand the math homework. What should you do?

_____

2. Your favorite movie is on TV late at night. What should you do?

_____

4 Drink: Complete the conversation. Write drink or drank.

Bill: I _____ one or two glasses of water a day.

Bob: You should _____ more water. It's good for you.

Bill: How much water did you _____ yesterday?

Bob: Me? I _____ six glasses of water. Big ones!

Grammar Handbook Practice

1 **Regular and Irregular Verbs in the Past:** Check the boxes.

	regular	irregular			regular	irregular
1. talk	☐	☐		5. hunt	☐	☐
2. go	☐	☐		6. disappear	☐	☐
3. study	☐	☐		7. do	☐	☐
4. have	☐	☐		8. drink	☐	☐

2 **Regular and Irregular Verbs in the Past:** Complete the sentences.

1. (live) The dinosaurs _____ for more than 160 million years.

2. (eat) Some really big dinosaurs _____ only plants.

3. (die out) The dinosaurs _____ about 65 million years ago.

4. (get) Some people think the weather _____ too cold.

3 **Question Formation:** Write a question with *is*, a question with *was*, and a question with *were*. Use at least one question word.

The Verb *Be*			
question word	form of *be*	subject	rest of sentence
	Are	pandas	in danger?

4 **Question formation:** Write a question with *do*, a question with *does*, and a question with *did*. Use at least one question word.

Other Verbs				
question word	auxiliary verb	subject	verb	rest of sentence
Why	did	ibexes	die out	in the year 2000?

Grammar Handbook Practice

1 **Simple Past:** Complete the past forms.

Regular: *live*

I _____   We _____

You _____   You _____

He/she/it _____   They _____

Irregular: *eat*

I _____   We _____

You _____   You _____

He/she/it _____   They _____

2 **Simple Past:** Change the affirmative verb forms to the negative.

1. In the past, people *had* running water. _____

2. People *used* phones to communicate. _____

3. People *listened* to CD albums. _____

4. People *rode* buses to school and work. _____

3 **Simple Past and *Used to* + Verb:** Underline the meaning.

1. We went to the soccer game.   one single finished action   habit in the past, not now

2. Laura used to live in Canada.   one single finished action   habit in the past, not now

3. Pat used to walk to school.   one single finished action   habit in the past, not now

4. I climbed a tree in the park.   one single finished action   habit in the past, not now

4 ***Used to* + Verb:** Write *used to* or *use to* + verb.

1. (cook) Before stoves, what did people _____ on?

2. (have) Lily _____ two rabbits. Now she has seven!

3. (ride) People didn't _____ in cars. Now they do.

4. (write) Students didn't _____ in notebooks. They had slates.

5. (sleep) I _____ in my sister's bedroom. Now I have a bedroom.

6. (like) George _____ folk music. Now he likes hip-hop.

7. (read) Before electricity, how did people _____?

8. (make) People _____ toothpaste with stone and vinegar.

Grammar Handbook Practice

1 **Future Plans and Intentions:** Which sentence talks about the future? Check.

1. ☐ Where's Lisa? She's cleaning her room.
2. ☐ Karen is going to have a party.
3. ☐ This afternoon, I'm helping Mom make dinner.
4. ☐ I'm going to the beach now.

2 *Be* + *going to* + **Verb:** Complete the sentences.

1. (do) What _____ Jenny _____ on Saturday?

   (play tennis) Jenny _____.

2. (buy) What _____ Jim and Judy _____ at the mall?

   (buy) They _____ new jackets.

3. (go) Where _____ you _____ for your vacation?

   (visit) I _____ my family in Miami.

4. (plant) _____ you _____ a tree on Earth Day?

   (clean up) No, I _____ the park that day.

3 **Ordinal Numbers:** Write the ordinal numbers.

1. 3rd _____   4. 16th _____

2. 1st _____   5. 22nd _____

3. 47th _____   6. 50th _____

4 **Dates and Plans:** What is the date of your birthday? What are you going to do?

_____

_____

_____

_____

Grammar Handbook Practice

1 *It's* + **Adjective** + **Infinitive:** Write sentences.

1. (exciting/play chess) _____

2. (fun/build model cars) _____

3. (boring/sew clothes) _____

4. (silly/collect rubber bands) _____

2 **Comparisons with Adjectives:** Write the comparative and superlative forms.

1. tall   → _____   → _____

2. big   → _____   → _____

3. easy → _____   → _____

4. large → _____   → _____

3 **Comparisons with Adjectives:** Write complete sentences.

1. Sandra is ten. Mark is eleven.

   (young) _____

2. Sandra is ten. Mark is eleven. Tina is twelve.

   (old) _____

4 *Good* and *bad:* Write the comparative and superlative forms.

1. good → _____   → _____

2. bad   → _____   → _____

5 **Comparisons with** *good* and *bad:* Write complete sentences about the boys' grades.

1. Johnny got 90% on his test. Greg got 60% on his test.

   (good) _____

2. Johnny got 90% on his test. Greg got 60% on his test. Sam got 45% on his test.

   (bad) _____

Grammar Handbook Practice

1 **Expressing Opinions:** Complete the sentences with your opinion.

| awesome | beautiful | boring | fun | hard | silly |

1. It _____ sing at parties.

2. I _____ ballet _____.

3. It _____ collect string.

4. I _____ hip-hop _____.

2 **Expressing Opinions:** Complete the question and write your opinion.

1. (ballroom dancing)

   What _____ you _____ of _____?

2. I think _____.

3 **Nouns as Adjectives:** Write noun + noun combinations.

| diet | fan | fruit | pencil | piano | video |

1. _____ game   4. _____ case

2. _____ dance   5. _____ salad

3. _____ lesson   6. _____ soda

4 *Would like:* Complete the questions and then write answers.

1. _____ you _____ to dance?

   _____

2. _____ Kate _____ to learn how to swim?

   _____

3. _____ you _____ a chili pepper?

   _____

4. Where _____ Kim _____ to go one day?

   _____

Prewriting

1 Practice choosing topics to write about. Complete the sentences.

1. One important thing in my life is _____.

2. One of my favorite _____ is _____.

3. When I look at the world, I think about _____.

2 Let's say you decide to write about *food*. Food is just too big to write about. You could never write everything there is to say about food! So now you have to focus your topic and think of different, smaller ideas about food you could write about.

food → Mexican food → my favorite Mexican dish

Make these big topics smaller so that they are the right size to write about.

music →

games →

3 Now try another way to get ideas about your topic. Choose *music* or *games* or a topic of your own and answer the questions.

Who?   _____

What?   _____

When?   _____

Where?   _____

Why?   _____

4 Your topic is *the ocean*. Fill in the word map with different ideas.

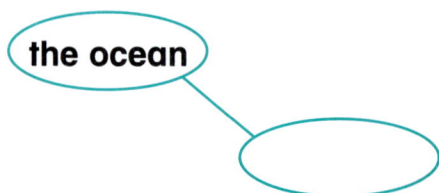

Writing the First Draft

1 Look at the list of topics. Choose three.

books	chores	computers	deserts	friends	holidays
hurricanes	libraries	money	moving	stars	transportation

Focus each of your three topics and make it the right size to write about. Write your three focused topics on the lines.

_____   _____   _____

2 Write a different beginning for each focused topic.

Interesting fact _____

Quotation _____

Question _____

3 Plan the middle part of your writing for each of the three topics. Circle a word and then complete your idea. Look at the example.

Sample Topic: I want to (describe) explain convince compare
my favorite toy when I was six years old,

Topic 1: I want to describe explain convince compare

_____

Topic 2: I want to describe explain convince compare

_____

Topic 3: I want to describe explain convince compare

_____

4 Plan and write a different ending for each of your three topics.

_____

_____

_____

Revising

1 Read the first draft about sloppy uncle David carefully. Decide how you want to change it. Ask yourself questions to help you decide.

1. Do I want to add more ideas or details?
2. Do I want to take out any sentences?
3. Is there a clear beginning, middle, and end?
4. Do I need to change the order of some sentences?
5. Do I need to change some words or sentences?

> I hate to say it, but my mom is right. It's important to be neat and clean up after yourself. How do I know? I'm going to tell you about my uncle. I went to stay with my uncle David in his small apartment for a week. I love my uncle, but he's really sloppy. When I entered, there was some sort of old or sour smell I couldn't identify. I figured it out when I saw all the dirty clothes on his chairs, bed, and floor. And not just his clothes. I saw old pizza delivery boxes and cereal boxes and candy wrappers and half-empty soda cans all over. I saw dirty dishes piled in the sink. His dishes weren't the only pile. I saw his sports equipment was all thrown into a big pile in one corner. I saw his newspapers and magazines were all in a pile in another corner. How can he find anything? And I saw his desk had piles of papers and bills on it. How can he live like that? I know now that I definitely don't want to!

2 Make changes. Write any sentences or sentences you change on the lines below. Cross out any words or sentences you want to take out in the draft above. If you change the order of a sentence, underline it and draw an arrow to show where you want to move it.

_____
_____
_____
_____
_____

3 Write a good title for the revised paragraph.

_____

Editing and Proofreading

1 Read the first draft below. Decide if you need to change any sentences for style, grammar, punctuation, spelling, or capitalization.

> Everyone loves pandas. They are in danger of disapearing from the planet. The most big threat to pandas is humans. Some people cut down the bamboo forests. pandas use them for food. They need to eat enormus amounts of bamboo every day. It isn't very nutritious. Some people hunt them for food. Some kill them for their fur. Leopards sometimes kill pandas to. Others build towns where pandas like to live, and so they have to leave. They're favorite habitat are cool, wet, mountain forest land. Another reason pandas are in danger is that they like to live alone most of the time They don't have very many babys. If a mother has two cubs, usually only one lives. The bears we love because they are so cute will one day live only in a few zoos around the world.

2 Underline the parts you think you want to change. Then write a second draft of the paragraph with your changes.

_____

_____

_____

_____

_____

_____

_____

_____

_____

_____

_____

_____

Publishing

1 Choose an animal from the list.

ant	bat	crocodile	dog	goat	horse	lion
monkey	ostrich	panda	rat	snake	tiger	worm

2 You are going to write a little poem about your animal. The poem has five lines, and it has a diamond shape. That means your longest line is in the middle, with shorter lines above and below. Look at the examples.

Camel

Always busy
carrying loads for others,
the camel glides through burning
sand, wishing you had a
hump on *your*
back too.

Frog

A splashy type,
good jumps and moves,
bullfrog grabs his microphone
and croaks out the
noise of rock
and roll.

3 Write your poem on paper. Check grammar and spelling. Cut the paper into a diamond shape. Sign your name.

4 Tape your animal poem and your classmates' poems to the classroom wall in one long line around the room.

5 Read your poem aloud to the class.

6 You're published!